GUEMES

RECIPES THROUGH THE YEARS

ISBN: 9798332879838

GUEMES ISLAND
RECIPES THROUGH THE YEARS

BROUGHT TO YOU BY
THE GUEMES ISLAND HISTORICAL SOCIETY

The Guemes Island Historical Society
Guemes Island. Washington

Acknowledgements

My heartfelt gratitude to the 100 cooks willing to share their favorite time-tested family favorites. Your contributions have helped create this unique collection reflecting the ethnic diversity and bounty of the land and waters surrounding Guemes. Thank you to the Washington Rural Heritage and the Guemes Island Historical Society for providing historical, 'food related' photographs. It has been a delightful learning experience going through both collections.

Thanks to Bud Ashbach, for never complaining about the computer and piles of recipes filling our dining table for months.

Thank you, Joseph Miller, for supporting me and to pull it all together. Your patience is legendary; your depth of knowledge, unbounded.

- Dawn Ashbach

Introduction

A Short History

Islands are magical. In few other places is this more apparent than in the Pacific Northwest, where a cluster of geologic jewels, the San Juan Islands, lie scattered in an emerald inland sea. In this exquisite setting, the geology, the climate, the natural beauty and human history have combined to form the San Juan Islands culture. The islands we see today are actually left over mountain tops from an ancient range. During the Ice Age, which ended about 12,000 years ago, glaciers covered and carved through the region, leaving behind a maze of waterways punctuated by some 172 islands (depending on the tide.) The Salish Sea, supports a rich food chain that extends from tiny protozoa, salmon, white fish, herring and octopus to whales. The shores offer clams, oysters, mussels and crab. The rich bounty of the sea and land provide the natural ingredients for fresh, mouthwatering recipes.

Spanish explorers, aboard the *Sutil* and the *Mexicana* recorded the first European sighting of the inhabitants of Guemes Island in 1792.

> "We saw a village close to the northwest point and upon examining it with the telescope, found it to consist of two large houses. Several Indians ran down to the beach, got into a canoe and steered for the schooner. In it an old man and four young ones of pleasant appearance came boldly alongside and gave us bramble berries. We gave each a metal button and they repeated their gifts in small portions to obtain something else in exchange...They also gave us dried shell fish of the sort sailors call verigones, threaded on a cord of bark. We accepted a sufficient quantity of them and also obtained a blanket of dog's hair, quilted feather's and a tanned deer hide."(1)

At this time, Guemes was named after the Viceroy of Mexico, Juan Vicente de Guemes Pacheco de Padilla Horcasitees y Aguayo Conde de Revilla Gigendo, who had funded the expedition. The Samish called the island, Qwengqwengíla, meaning 'lots of dogs' island. Using a whorl, the dog's fur was spun and used in weaving.

Contact with the 'foreigners' was limited to trade until the early 1840's when extensive settlement began in the Puget Sound area. United Sates government population figures show a 92% population lost between the years 1847 and 1855, reducing the population to 150. It is thought this loss was due to epidemics of small pox, measles and raids from northern tribes.

According to Charlie Edwards, a Samish leader and informant for Wayne Suttles, many of the Old Guemes villagers moved to the north shore of Fidalgo island where a fort was built. This village and the Old Guemes village (near the southwest point of Guemes) were probably completely abandoned by 1850 when they moved to Samish Island. (2)

The area historically used by the Samish tribe was ceded to the United States in the Treaty of Point Elliot, which was signed in 1855 and ratified in 1859. This was one of a series of treaties negotiated by Governor Isaac Stevens with Washington Indian Nations to provide property for white settlement. They agreed to the land cession in return for the right to maintain hunting, fishing and gathering rights on all open and unclaimed lands, plus the anticipation of reservation land. The Samish were not mentioned in the final draft, as they were considered to be covered by the signature of the Lummi 'chief.' There being little connection between the two tribes, the Samish remained on Samish Island until pressure by white settlers led to their moving to March Point in 1869 in anticipation of being given reservation land there. When this did not happen, they relocated to the site of the New Guemes village about 1875.

The New Guemes village was on the west shore of Guemes facing Bellingham Channel. It was built on land that was homesteaded by Harry Watchoat and Billy Edwards under the Indian Homestead Act of 1875. (3) Lucius Blackinton and James Matthews where the 'white' men who cosigned the land agreement on April 5, 1876, giving Watchoat and Edwards 232 acres. A long house was built using cedar shakes. It measured 480 feet long and 40 feet wide, built along the dividing line of the two lots. Nine men built the house and lived there with their families: Sam Watchoat, Billy Edwards, Harry Whulholten, Barney Whulhoten, Bob Edwards, Charlie Edwards, Dick Edwards Tommy Bibb and Kowigian. The permanent population was 55, but often as many as 100 were in residence.

While the villages located on Guemes and Samish Islands provided their permanent home, summer residences were throughout the San Juan Islands where they had fishing and hunting spots. (4) The New Guemes village started to decline about 1900, but ceremonial use of the land continued until the land was sold sometime between 1907 and 1910. This decline may be attributed to the loss of the rights to important fishing grounds, plus restrictions on fishing that occurred around 1900, taking away their means of making a living. Another possible cause was the expiration of the trust period on the homestead land, which would have expired in 1901. Some Samish moved to the Swinomish Reservation, some chose off-reservation and some remained on Guemes.

In 1996, the Samish were officially re-recognized by the U.S government and officially changed their name to the Samish Indian Nation. Today's population is 1,200 and have acquired more than 360 acres of their traditional territory.

- Dawn Ashbach

Wayne P. Suttles, *Coast Salish and Western Washington Indians I, The Economic Life of the Coast Salish of Haro and Rosario Straits.* (New York: Garland Publishing 1974, pages 246-7.
Ibid, page 43
Ibid, page 45
Ibid, page 41

Introduction

GUEMES ISLAND

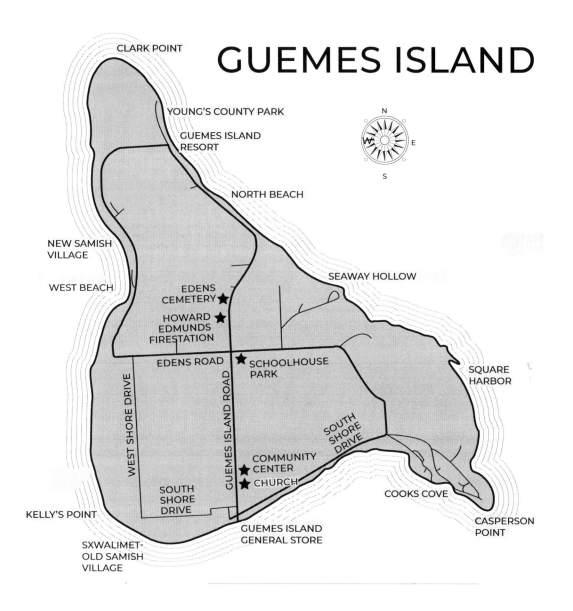

CLARK POINT

YOUNG'S COUNTY PARK

GUEMES ISLAND
RESORT

N

W   E

S

NORTH BEACH

NEW SAMISH
VILLAGE

WEST BEACH

SEAWAY HOLLOW

EDENS
CEMETERY ★

HOWARD ★
EDMUNDS
FIRESTATION

EDENS ROAD   ★ SCHOOLHOUSE
PARK

SQUARE
HARBOR

WEST SHORE DRIVE

GUEMES ISLAND ROAD

SOUTH
SHORE
DRIVE

COMMUNITY
CENTER ★
★ CHURCH

COOKS COVE

SOUTH
SHORE
DRIVE

KELLY'S POINT

CASPERSON
POINT

GUEMES ISLAND
GENERAL STORE

SXWALIMET-
OLD SAMISH
VILLAGE

Contents

Appetizers

Guemes Island Labor Day BBQ, 1956

Gruyére Cheese Dip

"The Sheridan family is known for their delicious additions to West Beach potlucks."

1 8-ounce package light cream cheese
8 ounces shredded Gruyere cheese
6 scallions, chopped, including greens
1 cup sliced cooked mushrooms, if desired

1. Preheat oven to 375 degrees.
2. In a medium bowl, mix all ingredients. Place in a shallow pie plate.
3. Bake 20 to 30 minutes, until bubbly and edges are crispy. Serve with crackers and enjoy!

- Meghan Sheridan

Reuben Dip

"In the fall, a group of men get together at the Ashbach's to make cider, from island apples and sauerkraut from the huge cabbages, grown in the Skagit Valley. The 'male bonding' group produces a lot. Always good to find one more tasty sauerkraut recipe."

8 ounces sliced corned beef, diced
2 cups sauerkraut, drained
8 ounces shredded Swiss cheese
8 ounces shredded cheddar cheese
1 cup mayonnaise

1. Preheat oven to 350 degrees. In a large bowl, mix together all ingredients.
2. Transfer to an oven safe baking dish (9"x13").
3. Place baking dish on a rimmed cookie sheet and bake for 30 minutes or until light brown and bubbly. Serve with Tostitos Scoops or other crackers.

- Nancy Bush

Tara's Dip

"Delicious with ribbed potato chips. Excellent on sliced baguette with smoked salmon, red onion and capers."

1 8-ounce package cream cheese, room temperature
2 tablespoons of mayonnaise
1/2 teaspoon garlic salt
2 English cucumbers, diced
4 chopped scallions

1. In a medium bowl, mix all ingredients. Chill and serve.

- Tara Dowd

Rancho del Valle Guacamole

"Make this yummy guacamole just before serving. Serve in a colorful bowl with tortilla chips."

3 ripe avocados, Fuerte or Hass
1 lime, juiced
1/2 medium red onion, diced
1 Roma tomato, seeded, diced and drained
2 garlic cloves, finely chopped
2 tablespoons cilantro, or parsley
Red pepper flakes, to taste
Salt, to taste

1. Cut avocados in half, discard seeds. Scoop out center with soup spoon and place in bowl. Add lime juice, onion, tomato, garlic, cilantro, red chili pepper flakes and salt.
2. Using a fork, mash all together.

- Carol Steffy
3 to 4 cups

Eggplant, Capers and Red Pepper Appetizer

"Pre-cooking the eggplant in a microwave is a real time saver."

2 medium eggplants

1/4 cup extra virgin olive oil, more as needed

Salt and pepper

Garlic powder (real minced garlic works, but prone to burn)

Red chili flakes, to taste

1/2 cup capers, drained

1 red bell pepper, finely chopped

Balsamic vinegar glaze

Fresh basil, chopped

1. Preheat oven to 400 degrees. Clean eggplants and cut off both ends. Slice each in half lengthwise, then cut in half again lengthwise, leaving four roughly one-inch "steaks" from each eggplant, eight total. Four will have significant skin on them and be rounded on top..

2. Arrange eggplant steaks on a plate and microwave on high for five minutes. This process is quicker than "salting and sweating" the eggplants.

3. While microwaving eggplant, cover a large sheet pan with aluminum foil and liberally oil to prevent sticking.

4. Pour olive oil into a small bowl and get out a brush.

5. Arrange microwaved eggplant steaks on oiled sheet pan and brush top with oil. Season with salt, pepper, garlic powder and red chili flakes, to taste. Sprinkle with capers and red bell pepper. Drizzle with a little more olive oil.

6. Bake at 400 degrees for about 20 minutes. Turn oven to broil and broil for about 5 minutes until you get a bit of char. Remove from oven, drizzle with balsamic vinegar glaze. Top with basil.

7. Cool for 5 minutes and slice diagonally. It can be finger food by itself or served on crackers.

- Eric Veal

Easy, Tasty Appetizer

"An easy, simple, tasty appetizer to please the most discerning tastes."

Como bread, sliced

Pesto

Pancetta or speck

Fresh mozzarella, room temperature

1. Preheat oven to 350 degrees. Place bread on a baking sheet, place in oven for five minutes, flip over and paint with pesto.
2. Layer bread with pancetta (or speck). Top with clumps of mozzarella.
3. Return to oven until cheese melts. Finish under broiler to slightly brown, about 2 minutes.
4. Top with red pepper flakes, as desired. Serve warm.

- Matt Ashbach

Cod Balls

"Jo Ann Shoemake's family bought Bubble's home sometime in the 1980's. Her Cod Balls became a tradition with her family and friends on Lervick Avenue." Bob Porter shared, "Bubble's doctor said she had 6 months to live, so Shoemake's told her she could live out her life in her home. Sixteen years later, she passed away."

Cod, patted dry

Krusteaz Bake and Fry Batter

Cold water

Oil

1. Cut cod in small pieces. Whisk batter with water until the consistency of pancake batter.
2. Coat cod, one piece at a time to be sure each piece is completely coated. .
3. In a large skillet, over medium-high, heat oil.
4. Cook in small batches, 4 to 5 pieces. Deep fry 2 to 4 minutes until cooked and golden brown. Remove to drain on paper towels. Serve hot.

- Marge Kilbreath

Bud's Dilly Beans

"These are a favorite appetizer and also delicious in a Bloody Mary. Can beans in late August when beans are garden fresh."

2 pounds green beans

2 1/2 cups water

1 teaspoon cayenne pepper, divided

2 1/2 cups vinegar

4 garlic cloves, peeled and sliced

1/4 cup canning salt (non-iodized)

4 heads of fresh dill weed

1. In 4 sterile pint jars, pack beans lengthwise. To each jar, add 1/4 teaspoon cayenne, 1 sliced garlic clove and 1 head of dill.

2. In a large pot, combine water, vinegar and salt and bring to a boil. Pour into each jar, covering beans, completely.

3. Tighten sterile canning lids on jars. Fill a large pot with hot water. Place jars in pot being sure water covers the tops. Boil for 10 minutes.

4. Remove and place on a towel to cool. For full flavor, wait at least one month before enjoying. Store in a dark, cool room.

- Bud Ashbach

4 pints

Crab Strudel

"A favorite summer appetizer, it's a labor of love, and well worth it."

1 package frozen phyllo dough, 10 sheets

12 tablespoons (1 1/2 sticks) unsalted butter, divided

3 scallions, sliced

2 garlic cloves, minced

1 teaspoon curry powder

1 pound Dungeness crab, cooked

2 teaspoons parsley, chopped

1 lime, juiced

Salt and pepper, to taste

1/4 cup plain dry bread crumbs

1. Remove one package of phyllo from freezer. Defrost according to package directions. (There are two packages in a box.)

2. Preheat oven to 400 degrees. In a medium saute pan, over medium low heat, melt 2 tablespoons butter. Sauté scallions and garlic, about 5 minutes, add curry powder and blend. Set aside.

3. In a medium bowl, shred crab meat, add parsley, lime juice, salt and pepper. Add scallion mixture and mix.

4. In a small pan, melt remaining 10 tablespoons butter and set aside.

5. Unfold 1 sheet of phyllo, brush with melted butter and sprinkle with about 1 teaspoon bread crumbs. Repeat process by laying a second phyllo sheet over the first, until 5 sheets have been used.

6. Spoon a 1-inch wide row of crab mixture along the longer edge of the phyllo stack. Roll up, brush the top with melted butter. Repeat using all phyllo and crab, making 4 rolls.

7. Cover a sheet pan with parchment paper and place rolls. Score each strudel, half way through, diagonally into 1 1/2 inches pieces.

8. Bake for 12 minutes, or until the top is lightly browned. Let cool for 10 minutes, slice and serve.

- Meghan Sheridan

Smoked Salmon with Rosemary Glaze

"Smoking salmon has been a joint venture between my son, Gabe and me. It has been a Murphy family tradition for over 40 years. I want to give credit and many thanks to an old friend, Bob Leatherwood, for allowing me to carry on this well-loved Guemes tradition."

Salmon, 5 to 6 pounds
Rock salt (American Stockman Solar Medium Salt, Kiln Dried)
Little Chief Smoker
Dry apple wood chips (Or other fruit wood, do not use green wood.)

While fish is in Smoker, prepare Rosemary Glaze, see recipe below.

1. Filet fish and cut into 2-inch wide pieces, making sure to remove belly skin. If you prefer, you can "slime" the fish first. I find it unnecessary for Sockeye. (If using Dogs, Kings or Humpies, then slime.)

2. Prepare a Rubbermaid dishwashing basin, or other 12 X 18 X 6 container, by setting down a thick layer of salt. Place fish, flesh side up, on top of the salt. Place a second layer of salt and then fish with flesh side down. Continue alternating layers until the basin is near full. Finally place a layer of salt on top. Layers of salt should be just enough to cover the fish. Leave fish and salt to sit for 2 1/4 hours.

3. Rinse the fish thoroughly under cold running water, maybe 5-6 times.

4. Prepare and clean drying boards (2 X 4 foot boards). Place fish on boards, leaving some space in between each filet. Place the boards on an incline. Place an oscillating fan in front of the boards, and air dry the filets for 6- 8 hours, until they have a nice shiny sheen.

5. Be sure to pre-heat your smoker, getting the chips to produce smoke. Once the smoker is ready, place fish on the smoker trays. The goal is to bring the internal temperature of the fish up to an initial internal temperature of 130 degrees. Depending on the outside temperature, it usually takes my smoker 5 to 6 hours to heat up to 130 degrees.

6. Once the temperature is reached, remove the fish trays, and apply the Rosemary Glaze to the filets. Place fish back in the smoker until the internal temperature of the fish reaches 140 – 145 degrees. I use a digital thermometer.

7. Remove smoked fish. Place on wax paper, keeping filets separate, until cooled. You can then refrigerate or freeze – or eat the fish! We usually can't wait for the fish to cool before we give it a try!

Rosemary Glaze

"Bob Leatherwood, former Guemes Ferry Captain, shared this delicious glaze with me in the early 1980's."

3 8-inch sprigs fresh rosemary, chopped fine, use more if dried.
1 cup extra virgin olive oil
1 cup light brown sugar

8. In a medium saucepan, combine rosemary and olive oil.
9. Bring to a simmer and cook for 15 minutes. Let cool and stir in sugar. Don't add sugar to hot oil or you will have a carmelized glaze, which you don't want.

- Mike Murphy

Yields enough glaze for 4 5-pound salmon.

Happy Hour Dungeness Crab

"We enjoyed this appetizer on our many island vacations. Now that we live here, we can enjoy more often. Serve on baguette toasts, or tortilla chips along with guacamole and hopefully margaritas! Or cold beers."

3 tablespoons butter

1 cup chopped red onion

2 cloves garlic, chopped

3 medium heirloom tomatoes, chopped into bite size chunks, drained

1 poblano chili, diced

1 pasillo chili, chopped

Achiote paste, prepared or homemade, to taste

1 cup coriander or flat-leaf parsley, minced

2 cups (16-ounces) Dungeness crab, chunked

Salt and pepper, to taste

1 cup toasted bread crumbs, more as needed

1 cup Parmesan cheese, more as needed

1. Preheat oven to 350 degrees. In a large skillet, melt butter and sauté onion and garlic, until wilted. Add tomatoes, chilis, and achiote paste, cook down.
2. Stir in coriander and crab, heat through.
3. Portion 1/3 cup of crab mixture into 6 ramekins; cover each with toasted bread crumbs and parmesan cheese.
4. Place ramekins on cookie sheet in oven, for 5 minutes, or until crab mixture hot and cheese is melted and toasted.

- Carol Steffy

Mike Murphy's Famous Smoked Salmon Dip

"It all started with Bob Leatherwood. Remember Bob – Past Guemes Ferry Captain, North Beach resident and all-around amazing human being. Bob shared his recipe for smoking salmon with me years ago, sometime in the 1980's. When he passed away, his famous smoker was gifted to me and that began our annual ritual of acquiring the freshest fish, smoking and freezing it, and always making a huge bowl of Smoked Salmon Dip. This Smoked Salmon Dip has fed folks all over Guemes Island, all the way down to the Bay Area in California, and has earned a famous secret nickname – but we will just call it "addictive!

In the early days (1980-ish) we would begin the process in the wee hours of the morning. We would grab our 5-gallon buckets and head down to West shore to meet our local fisherman and good friend, Arn Veal. We would receive a very early morning phone call telling us that he was coming in off the water and he had a "certain number" of fish and we better get down to the beach fast if we wanted some. It was a little like when the Guemes fire siren goes off and suddenly you hear cars revving down the road, coming from different directions – all racing to the beach to get fish from Arn. We barely had time to put on our boots! When we arrived at the beach, it looked like the parking lot down at the ferry landing – so many cars, sleepy men in hoodies and rubber boots, carrying white five-gallon buckets and coolers. Most of the time we got fish and even filled our coolers and buckets. Sometimes there was only one fish, which we had for dinner that night. And most of the time there was enough fish for everyone who showed up – but, if you didn't drive fast enough, you would be going home with an empty bucket. We still get the freshest fish, from local fisherman, and usually right off the boat, but we don't get up so early in the morning (or race down the road in the wee hours, in the dark, at high speeds!).

Once we had the fish, we would begin the process of gutting, filleting and air drying the fish, getting it ready to put in the smoker. Finally, we put together the secret ingredients to make the sauce that is brushed on the partially smoked salmon, and let the sauce simmer on the stove, filling the air with the smell of olive oil, brown sugar, and rosemary. This whole process takes a couple of days to complete and always ends with a "Smoker Party" where family and friends gather around the smoker sampling the fish as it comes right out of the smoker. Delicious! See recipe for 'Smoked Salmon with Rosemary Sauce' We hope you enjoy this Salmon Dip as much as our family does." - Michael, Charmaine, Gabe, Megan, Austin and Elise.

1 8-ounce package cream cheese (room temperature)

1 cup sour cream

1/2 cup mayonnaise

4 large green onions (or large handful of chives), chopped

4 large cloves of garlic, minced

1/4 cup fresh dill weed, chopped

1 cup smoked salmon (or more!)

Corn chips

1. In a large bowl, thoroughly mix all ingredients except salmon and corn chips.

2. Break up the smoked salmon into chunks, gently add to the cream cheese mixture, blending carefully so as not to break up the chunks of salmon too much.

3. We usually just start eating it, dipping our corn chips deeply into the bowl and scooping huge amounts into our mouths! But you can also refrigerate and let the flavors blend for an hour before serving. Sometimes the dip will last up to three days in the refrigerator, but most often it is shared with neighbors and friends and completely gone in a flash

- Mike Murphy

About 4 cups

North Beach Clam Dip

"This recipe was originally from my Croatian father-in-law, Augie. He would take our boys out clam digging at low tide. His motto was always, "any clam is a good clam." In addition to the steamers and butter clams, he would bring in cockles, mud clams, horse clams or whatever he found. My parents, John and Joyce Webber on West Beach, soon adopted it and served it at the cocktail parties popular at that time. It was always a hit. Recently, I have revived it at my husband, Tony's request. Still easy, still delicious."

8-ounce package cream cheese

1 6-1/2 ounce can minced clams, drained. (3/4 cup ground fresh, if the tide is low)

Juice of one lemon

3-4 green onions, finely sliced

2-3 dashes of Worcestershire Sauce

1/8 teaspoon pepper

Cayenne, to taste

1. In a medium bowl, use a hand mixer to thoroughly mix all ingredients. Refrigerate overnight to allow flavors to blend.

2. Remove from refrigerator at least an hour before serving. Serve with vegetables, tortilla chips, potato chips or pretzels.

- Jayne Mardesich

Maple Nut Party Mix

"Another Dianne Neilson family favorite. A sweeter version of the standard Chex Mix."

8 cups Crispix or mixture of Chex cereals

1 cup honey roasted cashews

1 cup honey roasted peanuts

1/4 cup margarine

1/3 cup brown sugar

2 teaspoons maple extract

1. In a large microwave-safe bowl, combine cereal and nuts.

2. In a small microwave-safe bowl, melt margarine in microwave; stir in brown sugar and maple extract.

3. Gradually pour over cereal and nuts, stirring until evenly coated.

4. Microwave all for 1 1/2 minutes, three separate times, totalling 4 1/2 minutes.

5. Spread on wax paper to cool.

- Dianne Neilson

10 cups

Simple Egg Rolls

"These are so easy, I make them often. They can be frozen and heated in a skillet for a quick lunch or snack. This is the basic recipe, but there is no end to the possibilities you can add. No eggs involved."

1/2 cup chopped celery

1/2 cup grated carrot

1 1/2 cup finely sliced cabbage

1/2 cup sliced almonds

1/2 cup frozen peas

2 or 3 green onions, chopped

1 1/2 cups cooked Jasmine rice

1 1/2 cups cooked and chopped chicken (or shrimp)

1 package egg roll wrappers

Vegetable oil, as needed

3 tablespoons soy sauce

1/2 cup sweet and sour pepper sauce

1. Place all vegetables in a bowl. Add rice and protein; mix all to combine.

2. Set up your egg roll wrappers with a small bowl of water, at hand.

3. Place the wrapper pointed up and down and put 1/3 cup of vegetable mixture in the middle. Fold the bottom point over the filling to meet with the top point, in the middle. Then fold the sides over to meet in the middle. Roll to seal and dab a bit of water on the top point to secure.

4. In a heavy pan, (I use cast iron) heat about an inch of vegetable oil. When hot, add rolls in, cook until brown on one side and then turn over. When both sides done, drain on paper towels.

5. Serve with soy sauce or pepper sauce for dipping.

- Cathy Schoenberg

Curried Quinoa Croquettes

"Joan had a passion for healthy cooking and loved sharing delicious meals with family and friends. She developed recipes while living on the island using fresh and vibrant ingredients often grown in her immense garden. These delightful treats make a perfect side dish or snack for any occasion. They not only are healthy but are packed with flavor. They freeze wonderfully, allowing you to enjoy them anytime. Simply pop them out of the freezer and heat them up in a pinch, and you'll have a convenient and delicious option ready for even the busiest of days."

1 1/2 cups quinoa or 1 cup millet cooked in 3 cups water

1/2 teaspoon salt

1-2 teaspoons curry powder

1/2 teaspoon thyme

2 cloves garlic

1/4 cup tahini

1 small onion, grated

1 cup grated rutabaga or winter squash

2 eggs

1/2 cup quinoa flakes

1. Cook quinoa or millet, according to package instructiosn, with salt, curry powder, thyme and garlic. When fluffy, stir in the tahini and grated vegetables.

2. Taste to correct seasoning.

3. Add eggs, stirring well.

4. Stir in the quinoa flakes.

5. Line cookie sheets with unbleached parchment and form small, balls with a spoon or your fingers. Fill each tray and bake at 375° for about 25 minutes or until the balls are firm and slightly browned.

Serve with dipping sauce, if desired.

Dipping Sauce

1/2 cup water

3 sprigs fresh mint

1 handful fresh cilantro

3 scallions, chopped coarsely

3 tablespoons almond butter

Juice of 1 lime

1/2 teaspoon salt

A few drops liquid stevia (optional)

1/2 jalapeño, seeded and chopped (optional)

Blend everything in a blender until smooth.

- Joan Miller

Hummus with Shallots and Shishito Peppers

"A perfect appetizer for happy hour on the beach. Serve with warm pita bread or pita chips."

2 to 3 tablespoons extra virgin olive oil

4 large shallots, thinly sliced

1/4 teaspoon salt

6 ounces shishito peppers, whole

2 cloves garlic, minced

1 teaspoon Aleppo pepper

1 teaspoon sumac spice

12 ounces homemade or store bought hummus

1. In a large skillet, heat olive oil until shimmering. Add the shallots and season with salt, shishito peppers and minced garlic.

2. Cook on high heat, undisturbed for 3 minutes. Reduce heat to medium high, cook 3 to 5 minutes more until the shallots and peppers have some nice charring, and the peppers are blistered and softened. Manage the heat to prevent burning.

3. Turn off the heat and season with a dash of salt, Aleppo pepper and sumac.

4. Spread hummus onto a plate. Make a wide, shallow well in the middle and drizzle some extra oil. Sprinkle with some sumac and Aleppo pepper.

5. Top with the charred shishito peppers and shallots.

- Terri Ramsay Reed

Salads

Guemes Island Labor Day Bar-B-Que, 1956

Pick-It Salad

"An Everett family favorite on North Beach. I learned about it from Billy's sister Susie and another North Beacher, Mugsy Duryee. They adapted it from their favorite Seattle restaurant, Canlis. The name is because you 'pick it' with your fingers."

2 heads baby Romaine

1/2 cup crumbled blue cheese, divided

1/2 bottle of your favorite Italian Vinaigrette, divided

1. Trim off woody ends and wash Romaine. Chill in cold water. Wrap in paper towels, place in plastic bag and refrigerate.

2. In a small bowl, mash 3 tablespoons of blue cheese and mix with 3 tablespoons of Vinaigrette. Mix to form a paste.

3. On a round platter, arrange Romain in a circle, with tips pointing toward the center. Divide the paste mixture between the Romaine hearts, spreading it down the middle of the leaves.

4. Drizzle with remaining vinaigrette and blue cheese.

- Karen Everett

10 plus servings

Picnic Potato Salad

"A great picnic salad, as it does not contain mayonnaise. Can be served hot, room temperature or cold."

1 pound fingerling potatoes

1 tablespoon salt

1 pound asparagus, cleaned with tough ends removed

8 tablespoons olive oil, divided

20 cherry tomatoes, cut in half

1 red onion, sliced

2 tablespoons balsamic vinegar

Salt and pepper, to taste.

1. In a large pot, bring salted water to boil. Cook potatoes until tender when pierced with a fork. Drain, and cut in half lengthwise. Place on one half of large rimmed baking sheet.

2. Preheat oven to 400 degrees. Cut asparagus into 1-inch pieces and add to potatoes, toss with 4 tablespoons of oil, salt and pepper. Roast for 20 minutes. Place in large serving bowl.

3. Add tomatoes and onion, balsamic vinegar and 4 tablespoon of olive oil and toss. Salt and pepper, to taste.

- Lindsay Ashbach

8 servings

Sweet Onion Salad

"A great no mayonnaise summer salad. It gets better the next day. Add julienned red bell pepper or carrots for added color."

3 large sweet onions, Walla Walla or Vildalia
1 bunch cilantro, stemmed and coarsely chopped
1/4 cup white vinegar
1 teaspoon salt, to taste
1/2 cup pitted kalamata olives, cut in half
1/2 cup crumbled Feta cheese
Olive oil

1. Slice onions 1/4 inch thick and place in bowl. In another bowl, combine cilantro, vinegar, salt, olives and cilantro, add to onions and toss.
2. Refrigerate for several hours tossing occasionally. Before serving, add Feta and sprinkle with olive oil.

- David McKibben

Serves 6

Guemes Island Gluk

"This recipe for 'Fruit Salad Dressing,' was renamed by Lervick Avenue resident and friend, Bubble. It will keep for a week and is delicious over fresh fruit."

1/2 pint whipping cream
1 4-ounce package cream cheese, cut into small pieces
1 1/2 tablespoons sugar
3 tablespoons mayonnaise
1 tablespoon Miracle Whip
1/4 cup maraschino cherries, sliced
1/2 tablespoon cherry juice, for color
Fresh fruit

1. In a small bowl, beat whipping cream. Stir in remaining ingredients and chill. Serve over fresh fruit.

- Miriam Morrison

2 cups

Christmas Kale Salad

"Pat Adams' kale salad was a big hit at the 2023 Christmas Community Center Potluck. The blend of sweet, sour and crunchy, makes it so flavorful."

1 bunch kale

2 teaspoons kosher salt

1/2 cup red onion, chopped

2 Granny Smith apples, peeled and diced

1 cup toasted pumpkin seeds, more if desired

2 cups dried cranberries

1 1/2 cups Gorgonzola cheese, crumbled (or substitute Feta)

3/4 cup Bragg vinegar

1/2 cup olive oil

1. Remove stems from kale, and chop leaves up to an inch or smaller. Massage chopped kale with salt. 'So eating kale won't feel like eating sandpaper.'

2. Add next five ingredients and mix well with the kale.

3. In a small bowl, whisk together vinegar and oil, add to salad and toss to coat.

4. Refrigerate for at least an hour or two, before serving.

- Pat Adams

Serves 6

Winter Salad

"A beautiful, bright, tasty salad on a cold, gray winter day."

Vinaigrette
2 tablespoons cider vinegar
1 tablespoon honey
1 tablespoon finely chopped shallots
1 1/2 teaspoons Dijon mustard
1 1/3 cups vegetable oil
Salt and pepper, to taste
2 heads of butter lettuce, cleaned and gently torn
1 1/2 cups glazed walnuts, store bought
1 Honey Crisp or Fuji apple, quartered, cored and thinly sliced
1 cup pomegranate seeds
1/4 cup tarragon leaves
1/2 cup (about 2 ounces) crumbled Stilton or Maytag blue cheese
Salt and pepper, to taste

1. In a medium bowl, whisk together, first 4 ingredients. Gradually whisk in oil, salt and pepper to taste. Set aside.

2. In a large serving bowl, place lettuce. Add vinaigrette, walnuts and apples; toss to coat. Season with salt and pepper. Garnish with pomegranate, tarragon and cheese.

- Meghan Sheridan

Serves 10

Perfect Kale Salad

"This quick and easy salad is my go-to for almost any meal, any time of year. It is savory and bright, the perfect way to eat kale. When I visit my friends on Guemes, this is the most often requested recipe."

Salad

2 bunches Lacinato kale

1/2 cup grated Pecorino Romano cheese

1. Remove the stems from the kale and finely chop, add to large bowl. Using your hands, massage the kale to 'break it down.'

2. Top with cheese and cooled croutons. Drizzle with half of the dressing and give it a good toss. Add the remaining dressing and toss again.

3. Let sit for 10-15 minutes so the flavors meld. The longer it sits, the better it gets.

Croutons

1/2 loaf sourdough boule or any crusty bread

Olive oil

Flakey salt

4. Preheat oven to 400 degrees. Tear bread into 1-inch cubes (tearing provides a lot of nooks for the dressing.) Toss cubes with a good drizzle of olive oil and spread in one layer on a sheet pan. Sprinkle with a big pinch of flakey salt and toast in the oven for 12-15 minutes or until golden brown.

Dressing

1 clove garlic

1/2 teaspoon salt

1/2 lemon, juiced

2 tablespoons champagne vinegar

1/3 cup extra virgin olive oil

Freshly ground pepper

5. Using a mortar and pestle, smash garlic and salt to form a paste. Add lemon and vinegars and let sit for a few minutes. Whisk in olive oil and finish with pepper. Taste and adjust as needed. (It should seem slightly salty and bright, it will mellow on the salad.)

- Kellie Kalvig

12 servings

Classic Potato Salad

"When I worked in the kitchen at Anderson Feed & Grain (now Guemes Island General Store) in the late 90s, my co-worker, Joyce Baker made potato salad that everyone raved about. Five gallon buckets would fly out of the kitchen in small batches. Sadly, Joyce passed in 2020, but her great sense of humor and amazing cooking skills live on. This is my version of her recipe. The secret is soaking the cooked potatoes in dill pickle brine as they cool."

5 medium russet potatoes, skins on

1 teaspoon salt

1/2 to 1 cup pickle brine, divided

6 large eggs,

1 teaspoon salt

1/2 tablespoon cider vinegar

Salt and pepper, to taste

1/2 to 1 cup Best Foods Mayonnaise

2 tablespoons French's mustard

Salt and freshly cracked pepper, to taste

3 medium green onions (scallions), sliced

2 large kosher dill pickles, finely diced (Claussen)

1. In a medium saucepan, cover potatoes with cold water, add salt. Bring to a boil, turn to low and simmer for 20 minutes. Cook until the potatoes are soft when pierced with a fork. Drain the water, rinse the potatoes with cold water. Drizzle potatoes, skins on, with pickle brine. Place in fridge and turn the potatoes over every 10 minutes, until cooled, so the brine penetrates both sides.

2. While the potatoes boil, place eggs in a small saucepan and cover with water. Add salt and cider vinegar. Bring to a boil; turn heat to low, and simmer gently for 5 minutes. Turn off heat and let eggs sit in hot water for another 5 minutes. Rinse with cold water and place eggs in fridge to cool.

3. When potatoes are cold, use a paring knife to remove skins. Chop into small cubes and place in a bowl. Drizzle with a bit more pickle brine and sprinkle with salt and pepper.

4. When eggs are cold, peel and finely dice; add to potato mixture.

5. Mix in mayonnaise and mustard and if dry, add a bit more mayonnaise. Adjust mayonnaise, mustard, salt and pepper to taste. Mix slightly, mashing the mixture.

6. Add in the green onions and pickles; adjust seasonings as desired.

- Karen McEachran Everett

Serves 8

Curried Chicken Salad

"A savory salad that is both sweet and little spicy. It has lots of crunch from grapes, cashews and celery. Poach or use an already cooked rotisserie chicken. A favorite at our family gatherings."

3/4 cup plain yogurt

3/4 cup mayonnaise (Best Foods of course)

1/4 cup of Dijon mustard (or 1 tablespoon of dried mustard)

1 to 2 tablespoons curry powder (S&B from Uwajimaya)

1 to 2 tablespoons lemon pepper

4 cooked chicken breasts, cooled and cut into 1/2" cubes

1/2 cup of diced celery

2 cups of red grapes

3/4 cup of golden raisins

1/2 cup of sweetened dried cranberries or cherries

16-ounces cooked rotini or bow tie pasta, rinsed in cold water

Salt and pepper, to taste

1. In a large bowl, whisk together first 5 ingredients. Add remaining ingredients and toss to coat.

2. You may need to add more yogurt or mayonnaise for the right creaminess.

3. Cover and refrigerate for at least 6 hours as the flavors will continue to develop. Salt and and pepper to taste before serving.

- J. Forrest Nelson

8 servings

Sweet and Sour Cole Slaw

"In 1947, Charlie and Alice Townsend bought property and started, 'Charlie's Guemes Island Fishing Resort.' Their one cabin rental, grew to six cabins. Alice had a small cupboard store stocked all the essentials. In 1972, I called to ask if she had anchovies, and indeed, she did. After Alice passed, Charlie married Mimi, and they continued to operate the resort until his passing in 1995." - Dawn Ashbach

1 medium head cabbage, chopped (about 4 cups)

1 large sweet onion, chopped

1 large green pepper, seeded and chopped

2 cups shredded carrots

1 4-ounce jar of pimientos, chopped

Dressing

2 cups pf granulated sugar

1 3/4 cups of apple cider vinegar

1 tablespoon of salt

1 tablespoon mustard seed

1 teaspoon celery seed

1. In a large bowl, combine first 5 ingredients.

2. In a small saucepan, mix Dressing ingredients and heat over low, stirring continuously, until sugar dissolves. Pour over cabbage mixture, combine, cover and refrigerate until cool.

- Mimi Townsend

Serves 8

Kathy's Salad Dressing

"This recipe changes every time I make it, but the main components usually stay the same. I will taste and adjust a bit to add sweetness or increase savory flavors."

1 shallot, finely diced

1/2 orange, juiced

1/2 lemon, juiced

1/2 cup hummus (sometimes a bit more)

1 teaspoon Dijon mustard

1 teaspoon honey mustard

1/2 teaspoon soy sauce

1 tablespoon fresh parsley, chopped

1 tablespoon fresh basil, chopped

1/4 teaspoon pepper

1 tablespoon seasoned rice wine vinegar (sometimes balsamic vinegar)

In a medium bowl, combine all ingredients and whisk together. Cover and refrigerate.

-Kathy Whitman

1 cup

Roasted Vegetable and Orzo Salad

"This is a Seaway Hollow and family favorite. So easy and so flavorful."

1 small eggplant, 3/4 inch diced
1 red pepper, 1 inch diced
1 yellow pepper, 1 inch diced
1 red onion, peeled and 1 inch diced
2-3 garlic cloves, minced
1/3 cup olive oil
1 1/2 teaspoon kosher salt
1/2 teaspoon freshly ground pepper
8 ounces orzo

Dressing
1/3 cup freshly squeezed lemon juice (~2 lemons)
1/3 cup good olive oil, preferably lemon olive oil
1 teaspoon kosher salt
1/2 teaspoon freshly ground pepper

Assemble
4 scallions, minced (white and green parts)
1/4 cup pignolis, (pine nuts) toasted
12 ounces good quality feta, 1/2 inch diced (not crumbled)
15 fresh basil leaves, chiffonade (cut into long strips)

1. Preheat oven to 425 degrees. Onto a large baking sheet, toss the eggplant, peppers, onion and garlic together with olive oil, salt and pepper. Roast for 40 minutes, until browned, turning once halfway with a spatula.

2. While vegetable mixture is cooking, cook the orzo in boiling salted water for 7 to 9 minutes, until tender. Drain and transfer to a large serving bowl. In a small bowl, whisk together all dressing ingredients and set aside.

3. Add the roasted vegetables to the pasta, scraping all the liquid and seasonings from the roasting pan into the pasta bowl. While still warm, add dressing and toss to coat.

4. Let cool to room temperature. Add scallions, pignolis, feta and basil. Check for seasoning and serve at room temperature.

- Terri Ramsay Reed

Serves 8

Salads

Chicken Rice-A-Roni Salad

"This salad recipe has been in my file since forever. Very good with salmon, cod, halibut and good to bring to a summer gathering. For best flavor, refrigerate for three days before serving."

1 box of Chicken Rice-A-Roni, prepared, omitting butter, cooled

2 chopped green onions

1/2 green pepper, chopped

1 cup chopped celery, or more

2 small jars marinated artichoke hearts, drained and chopped. Reserve marinade.

1/2 cup slivered almonds, or more

1/4 cup chopped black or green olives, or more

Dressing

1/2 teaspoon curry powder

1/2 to 3/4 cup mayonnaise

Reserved artichoke marinade

1. In a large bowl, combine first 7 ingredients.

2. In a small bowl, combine the dressing ingredients.

3. Stir in dressing; cover and refrigerate for three days before serving.

- Diane Wallace

Serves 4

Entrées

First Thanksgiving in the new Community Hall, 1914

Rug Hooker Beans

"My Grandmother, Ann Bessner, made these beans for her fellow Ladies Rug Hooking group gatherings. We still have a couple of her rug masterpieces in our home. These beans became a family favorite and were often served at picnics and 4th of July celebrations on North Beach of Guemes. The recipe was then passed down to my mother Annette, who then shared it with my wife Vicki when we got married. We always use my Grandmother Ann's cast iron Dutch oven to bake and serve them. Delicious!"

1 pound hamburger

3/4 pound thick cut bacon, sliced

1 onion, chopped

1 tablespoon chopped garlic

1 28-ounce can B&M baked beans

1 15-ounce can butter beans, drained

1 15-ouncecan red kidney beans, drained

1 15-ounce can green beans, drained

1 15-ounce can garbanzo beans, drained

1 15-ounce can wax beans, drained

1/2 cup ketchup

1/2 cup brown sugar

1 tablespoon dry mustard

1 tablespoon Worcestershire Sauce

2 tablespoons apple cider vinegar

1. In a large cast iron pan, sauté hamburger, bacon and onion until cooked through. Add garlic and saute one minute.

2. Mix in remaining ingredients and heat through. Cover and place into a preheated 325 degree oven and bake 2-3 hours until your kitchen smells heavenly. Serve and enjoy!

- Mark and Vicki Mitchell

12 servings

Linguine alla Cecca

"This simple and delicious dish is served at room temperature. Perfect with garden fresh tomatoes. For additional flavor, stir chunked Burrata mozzarella into cooked pasta before adding tomato mixture. Twenty five grape tomatoes, sliced in half, can be substituted for large tomatoes."

5 large tomatoes

1 garlic clove, sliced

1 cup freshly chopped basil

3 tablespoons olive oil

Red pepper flakes, as desired

Salt and pepper, to taste

12 ounces linguine

1. Drop tomatoes in boiling water for 1 minute. Remove, cool, peel, seed and coarsely chop. Place in a bowl, season with salt and pepper, if desired.
2. Mix in garlic, basil and seasonings. Set aside to marinate at room temperature for 2 hours.
3. Cook linguine according to package directions.
4. Place drained linguine on serving platter and top with tomato mixture.

- Sally Stapp

Serves 6

BBQ Sauce

"A flavorful barbecue sauce enjoyed by our family. We serve it on hamburgers and as a seasoning for beef stew."

1 2/3 cup ketchup

1/2 cup cider vinegar

1/4 cup brown sugar

1 teaspoon cumin

2 teaspoon smoked paprika

1 teaspoon pepper

1 teaspoon salt

Combine all ingredients in a heavy saucepan and simmer for 5 minutes. When cool, bottle and refrigerate.

- Kay Marie Pope

2 1/2 cups

Entrées

Prewitt's Cheese and Nut 'Neat' Loaf

"This loaf has been a family favorite entrée for Thanksgiving or Christmas dinner for several years now. Accompanied by the usual sides and a savory mushroom gravy, it makes a great vegetarian entree in place of the usual turkey."

1 1/2 cups walnuts

1/2 cup cashews

1 1/2 cups cooked brown rice

2 tablespoon butter

1 small onion, finely chopped

1 1/2 cups crimini mushrooms, finely chopped

1 ounce dried porcini mushrooms, soaked in hot water for 20 min, drained and chopped

1 tablespoon dried parsley

1/2 teaspoon dried thyme

1/2 teaspoon dried sage

2 large cloves of garlic, finely minced

4 large eggs, beaten

9 to 12 ounces grated cheese – cheddar, jack, swiss and fontina are all good

1 cup cottage cheese

1 teaspoon salt

Freshly ground black pepper

1. Preheat oven to 375 degrees. Butter a 9" x 9" baking dish.

2. Toast walnuts and cashews on a baking sheet until lightly browned, about 6 to 8 minutes. Chop fine with knife or food processor.

3. In a fry pan, over medium heat, melt butter. Add the onion and cook until translucent. Add mushrooms and cook until they are brown and liquid from mushrooms has reduced by half.

4. In a large bowl, combine all the ingredients: onions, mushrooms, etc.

5. Spoon the mixture into the buttered baking dish and smooth it down until it is level.

6. Bake until golden brown and firm to the touch, about 45-50 minutes.

7. Let cool in dish for 10 minutes, then cut into serving size squares.

- Lynn Prewitt

Serves 9

Party Polenta

"This is a perfect dish for a summer barbecue, whether it is Mexican or Italian themed."

6 cups water, or chicken stock

2 teaspoons salt

2 cups Bob's Red Mill Yellow Corn Polenta

Mexican Polenta

3 cups salsa

3 cups shredded Mexican cheese

Italian Polenta

3 cups Marinara or Bolognese sauce

3 cups shredded mozzarella

1/2 cup Parmesan

1. Preheat oven to 400 degrees

2. In a large, heavy bottomed pot, bring water or chicken stock to a boil. Add salt in polenta and reduce heat. Slowly cook for about 5 minutes, stirring to prevent bottom from scorching. Remove from heat cover and let sit. Preheat oven to 400 degrees.

3. Mexican Polenta: Grease a 9x13 inch baking pan. Spread half the polenta on the bottom of pan. Top with 1 1/2 cups salsa and top 1 1/2 cups cheese. Repeat layering starting with polenta.

4. Italian Polenta: Grease a 9x13 inch baking pan. In a bowl, combine mozzarella and Parmesan cheese. Spread half the polenta on the bottom of pan. Top with 1 1/2 cups marinara or bolognese sauce and top with cheese mixture. Repeat layering, starting with polenta.

5. Cover lightly with foil and bake 40 minutes, uncover, bake 20 minutes more. Can be served warm or room temperature.

- Dawn Ashbach

12 servings

Quinoa Vegetable Casserole

"A quick and healthy casserole to serve after a day on the beach with family and friends."

1 1/3 cups water, vegetable or chicken broth

2/3 cup quinoa

1 tablespoon butter

2 tablespoon vegetable oil

1 onion, chopped

1 red pepper, diced

1 orange pepper, diced

1 teaspoon cumin

1/2 teaspoon pepper

2 cans black beans, rinsed

1 cup frozen corn kernels

1 cup halved cherry tomatoes

1 cup shredded zucchini

1/2 cup grated Monterey Jack cheese

Additional cheese, as desired

1. In a large sauce pan, bring water (or broth) to boil, stir in quinoa. Cover and simmer 20 minutes, according to package directions. Preheat oven to 375 degrees.

2. In a large frying pan, heat oil and butter. Sauté onion and peppers. Stir in quinoa, cumin and pepper. Mix in black beans, corn, tomatoes and zucchini. Toss with cheese.

3. Pour into a greased 9x13 inch baking pan. Top with additional cheese, if desired. Bake for 30 to 40 minutes.

- Sue Stapp O'Donnell

Serves 8

Capellini With Gorgonzola Sauce

"A true food lover and chef, Bruce was an early follower of Julia Childs. His lifelong love of cooking came from his mom and growing up in an Italian neighborhood. "Her red sauce would take two days. Day one, she would cook onions, garlic and herbs in a broth with pork bones. Day two she would add the remaining ingredients and let it simmer all day." Originally printed in the Guemes Tide, 2012."

8 ounces cappellini, or angel hair pasta

1 tablespoon salt

3/4 cup chopped Gorgonzola cheese

3/4 cup grated Parmesan cheese

1 cup cream or half-and-half

1 teaspoon dried tarragon

White pepper and salt, to taste

2 tablespoon chopped fresh parsley

1. In a large pot, bring 2 quarts of water and salt to a boil. Add pasta and cook for 6 minutes.

2. While pasta is cooking, in a saucepan, combine the cheeses and cream; heat over low. Stir in tarragon and pepper.

3. When pasta is done, drain, reserving 1 cup of pasta water, and mix with the sauce. Add salt, to taste. Add pasta water to thin, as needed.

4. Serve in individual pasta bowls and top with parsley. Serve with additional Parmesan.

- Bruce Rooney

4 servings

Green Lasagne

"Traditionally, the Ashbach family serves this vegetarian lasagne on Christmas Day with roast beef, green salad and garlic bread for a yummy holiday meal. It originates from family in Montulo Lucca, Italy. Make a day ahead so flavors have time to meld."

1 cup pesto

6 cloves garlic, crushed

Olive oil, as needed.

1 to 2 cups pine nuts (pignoli), toasted

1 pound of fresh flat Italian beans, or fresh green beans, of your choice

4 medium baker potatoes, peeled and quartered

16 ounces lasagne pasta, broken into pieces

1 to 2 tablespoons salt, as desired

3/4 cup chopped parsley

1/2 cup freshly grated Parmesan Cheese (grate your own)

Salt and freshly ground pepper, to taste.

Freshly grated Parmesan, for table.

1. A couple days ahead, make a slurry of pesto, garlic and olive oil. The amount of olive oil is dependent on your pesto.

2. Preheat oven to 375. Spread pine nuts in a single layer on a cookie sheet. Toast until golden brown, turning once or twice. Watch carefully, as they can burn in seconds. Immediately remove from heat and transfer to a flat plate to prevent further cooking. This can be done ahead and refrigerated.

3. Blanche beans until tender-crisp, about 8 minutes. Beans should remain bright green. Drain and rinse with cold water to stop cooking. Pat dry and set aside.

4. Boil potatoes in enough water to cover until tender, about 15 minutes. Drain, cool and slice; set aside.

5. Boil pasta in salted water, *al dente*, according to package directions. Test two minutes before timer rings, don't overcook. Before draining, remove 1 cup of the water and set aside. This water is called "liquid gold, " the starch from pasta will help bind the flavors of ingredients and avoid the gummy feel and look. (This is a good idea when making any pasta dishes. And always be sure to salt the water before cooking pasta.)

6. In a large bowl, combine pasta, beans, potatoes, parsley, pine nuts, and Parmesan. Salt and pepper to taste. Toss with pasta water, as needed and I always sprinkle with more olive oil. (Pasta water and oil will continue to be absorbed.) Place in 13"x9"-inch backing dish. Lasagne may be covered and refrigerated at this time.

7. Bake, covered at 350 for 30 minutes; if refrigerated, bake 60 minutes. Toss before serving, add additional olive oil, salt and pepper, as desired.

- Dawn Ashbach

10 servings

Artichoke and Mushroom Lasagna

"Over the years, this mushroom and artichoke lasagna has been a favorite to serve at island potlucks and dinner parties, earning a place in the fond memories of friends and family alike. The tender layers of pasta and rich béchamel sauce, combined with a delicious blend of mushrooms and artichokes, create a hearty dish guaranteed to leave guests with satisfied bellies. Can be prepared one day ahead, covered and refrigerated."

Filling

2 tablespoons butter

1 pound of mushrooms, sliced

4 garlic cloves, minced

1 small yellow onion, chopped

1 cup grated Parmesan cheese

2 cups of marinated artichoke hearts, drained and coarsely chopped, or 2-8 ounce packages of frozen artichoke hearts, thawed, drained, and coarsely chopped.

1 cup dry vermouth

Salt and pepper, as desired

Béchamel sauce

4 1/2 tablespoons butter

4 1/2 tablespoons all-purpose flour

4 1/2 cups whole milk

1 1/2 cups grated Parmesan cheese

1/8 teaspoon ground nutmeg, more as desired

Salt and pepper, as desired

1 9-ounce package of no boil lasagna noodles

1 pound thinly sliced or grated mozzarella cheese, divided

1. Filling: In a large skillet, melt butter over medium-high heat. Add mushrooms, onion, and garlic; sauté until mushrooms release juices and begin to brown, about 7 minutes.

2. Add cheese, artichokes and vermouth. Cook until liquid is absorbed, stirring occasionally, about 10 minutes. Season with salt and pepper

3. Béchamel sauce: In a heavy bottomed saucepan, melt butter over medium-high heat. Add flour and stir 1 minute. Gradually whisk in milk. Reduce heat to medium and simmer until sauce thickens, about 20 minutes, stirring occasionally. Continue until sauce lightly coats spoon. Stir in 1 1/2 cups Parmesan. Season to taste with nutmeg, salt, pepper as desired. Preheat oven to 350 degrees.

4. Build lasagne: Spread 2/3 cup béchamel sauce over bottom of 13"x9"x2"-inch glass baking dish. Top with enough noodles to cover bottom of dish. Spread 1/4 of artichoke mixture over. Spoon 2/3 cup béchamel sauce over mixture. Top béchamel with 1/4 pound of mozzarella. Sprinkle with 3 tablespoons Parmesan. Top with enough noodles to cover. Repeat layering 3 more times,

finishing with a layer of noodles, then remaining béchamel. Sprinkle with remaining Parmesan.

5. Bake lasagna covered with foil 1 hour (or 1 hour 15 minutes if chilled). Remove foil. Increase temperature to 450°F. Bake lasagna until golden on top, about 10 minutes.

- Sue Roberts

8 servings

Pasta Olivetti

"Long time Guemes resident, Dorothy Bird, served this flavorful chicken recipe. Served over pasta, the flavor cannot be beat."

2 tablespoons olive oil

4 boneless chicken thighs, cut into pieces

10 kalamata olives, pitted

1 tablespoon capers

2 cloves garlic, minced

1 cup chicken stock

16 ounce package of farfalle pasta

2 tablespoons olive oil

10 cremini mushrooms, sliced

8 sun-dried tomatoes, soaked and sliced

1 tablespoon pesto or dried basil

1/2 cup tomato juice

Salt and pepper, to taste

1. In a large fry pan, heat oil and brown chicken. Add olives, capers, garlic and chicken stock. Simmer on low.

2. In a large pot, cook pasta according to package directions. Reserve 1 cup of pasta water and drain pasta. Set aside, cover with foil to keep warm.

3. In second fry pan, heat olive oil. Add sun dried tomatoes, basil, chicken mixture, and tomato juice. Simmer to reduce a bit. Mix in ingredients from first fry pan. Add pasta water as needed for desired consistency. Salt and pepper, to taste.

4. Ladle pasta iton pasta bowls and top with chicken sauce.

- Dorothy Bird

6 servings

Mustard Crusted Chicken

"Mark served this amazing chicken dish after an eight hour horse trail ride in eastern Washington. (Had to include it because, so good! -Dawn Ashbach) Serve with mashed potatoes for the amazing sauce."

1 3 1/2 pound chicken
2 tablespoons chopped garlic
2 tablespoons Dijon mustard
2 tablespoons dry white wine
2 tablespoons olive oil
1 tablespoon soy sauce
1 teaspoon Tabasco
1 teaspoon Herbs de Provence
1/2 teaspoon salt
Mashed potatoes

1. Preheat oven to 450 degrees.
2. Spatchcock chicken. (Cut out backbone, and smash flat.) Cut chicken in half and cut through all joints, to help cook evenly.
3. In a medium bowl, mix together next eight ingredients.
4. Coat chicken with mustard mixture and place skin side up in a heavy pan.
5. Bake for 10 minutes, reduce heat to 400 and cook for about 40 minutes or until juices run clear when pierced with a fork.
6. Remove from oven and let sit about 5 minutes. Cut up chicken with shears.
7. Place a couple chicken pieces on a mound of potatoes and top with sauce.

- Mark Siks

Serves 4

Pasta Carbonara

"This simple recipe is an easy dinner to please even the most picky eater. Who doesn't love bacon? The egg yolks give the sauce a creamy texture and golden color. Use Guemes farm fresh eggs and freshly grated Parmesan, for best flavor. Serve with a green salad and crunchy bread."

4 large egg yolks

2 large eggs

1/4 cup freshly grated Parmesan

Salt and pepper, as desired

Water

1 pound bucatini pasta

1 tablespoon salt

1 tablespoon olive oil

8 ounces bacon or pancetta

1 cup freshly grated Parmesan, to serve

1. In a mixing bowl, whisk together whole eggs, yolks and cheese. Season with a pinch of salt and pepper, set aside.

2. In a large pot, cook pasta in salted water 2 minutes less than package instructions. Just before pasta is finished, scoop out 2 cups of pasta water and set aside. While pasta is cooking, complete Step 3.

3. In a large Dutch oven, over medium high, heat oil, add pancetta, stirring occasionally. Fry until edges are crisp. With a slotted spoon, remove pancetta and place on paper towel to drain. Discard all but 3 tablespoons of fat from the Dutch oven.

4. Add 1 cup of the pasta water to the fat in Dutch oven and bring to a boil. Drain pasta in colander and place in Dutch oven with the hot water and fat; toss to coat. Finish cooking pasta until 'al dente,' about 2 minutes. Remove from heat.

5. Whisk 1/4 cup reserved hot pasta water into egg mixture. Slowly, pour mixture over pasta, stirring until cheese is melted and egg has created a glossy sauce. (I use heavy tongs.) A little at a time, thin the sauce with remaining pasta water, as needed until the consistency of heavy cream. (You probably will not use all the water.) Salt and pepper, to taste.

6. Add pancetta and toss, using tongs and place in pasta bowls. Serve with Parmesan cheese.

- Dawn Ashbach

4 servings

Smothered Pork Chops

"Matt made this yummy dish using Guemes grown pork. I am a bit leery of cooking pork chops as so easy to make them dry and tough. This recipe is a winner." - Dawn Ashbach

4 1/2-inch pork chops
Salt and pepper
1/3 cup all-purpose flour
3 tablespoons olive oil, divided
1 large onion, sliced
1 pound mushrooms, sliced
2 teaspoons Italian seasoning
1 3/4 cups chicken stock
3/4 cup heavy cream
Salt and pepper, to taste

1. Using paper towels, dry the chops. Salt and pepper both sides. In a small bowl, place flour and coat chops. Do not discard remaining flour.

2. In a large frying pan, over medium-high, heat two tablespoons of oil. Sear the chops on each side for 3 minutes or until they look golden. Turn down the heat to medium and cook a few minutes more, until they reach an internal temperature of 145 degrees. Remove from pan, leave remaining oil in pan.

3. In the same pan, heat oil and add remaining 1 tablespoon oil, if needed. Add the onions and mushroom and sauté until onions are translucent and mushrooms start to brown.

4. Add the seasoning and the reserved flour to the onion and mushrooms. Pour in the chicken stock and stir until it thickens. Blend in the cream. Add salt and pepper, as desired.

5. Place the pork chops back into the pan, including any liquid. Slowly heat, over medium.

- Matt Ashbach

4 servings

Beef Short Ribs Stoup

"After many attempts to recreate an extraordinary meal of short ribs served at a Portland restaurant, this recipe is close and so delicious in its own way. A family and friendship group favorite. Yum."

2 tablespoons oil

1 small onion, chopped

3 carrots, peeled and sliced

3 celery stalks, sliced

3 garlic cloves, minced

6 beef short ribs or 1 1/2 pounds stew meat

2 tablespoons flour

1 cup red wine

2 or 3 32-ounce containers of beef or bone broth (more for Stoup, less for Short Ribs with Gravy)

1 14.5-ounce can diced tomatoes, including liquid

1 bay leaf

1 tablespoon Herbs de Provence

6 mushrooms

2 pounds yellow potatoes, diced or 1/2 cup pearl barley

Salt and pepper, to taste

1. In a large pot, over low, heat oil and saute the onion, carrots, celery and garlic, until onion becomes translucent. With a slotted spoon, remove vegetables from pan and set aside.
2. Dust the short ribs (or stew meat) with flour. In the same pot, over medium-high heat, brown the meat. Add more oil as needed.
3. Add wine and allow it to boil and reduce, about 3 minutes.
4. Add broth, diced tomatoes, onion mixture and herbs, bring to a boil. Turn temperature down. Cook, uncovered, for 1 hour at a brisk simmer to reduce.
5. Cover pot, reduce temperature and simmer for another 2 hours.
6. At the start of the third hour, add mushrooms, potatoes or barley. Continue to cook on simmer until potatoes (or barley) are done, about 1 hour. Salt and pepper, to taste.

- Joseph Miller

Serves 4 to 6

If you want Short Ribs with Gravy: Follow directions 1 through 5. Pour ingredients through a colander, or sieve reserving broth mixture and meat separately. In a large skillet, melt 3 tablespoons of butter and slowly whisk in approximately 1/4 cup of flour, enough for a thick paste. (I prefer Wondra Quick Mixing Flour, you will use a bit less and it mixes very easily.) Slowly add broth a bit at a time, whisking constantly. Raise the temperature and simmer gravy for five minutes, stirring constantly with a whisk. Return beef and onion mixture to pot and heat through.

Everett Chateaubriand With Colman's Mustard Marinade

"When I first met Billy Everett in the 1980s and he brought me to his parent's home on the North Beach of Guemes Island, he dazzled me with his prowess at marinating and cooking the family's favorite steak. The BEST I've ever had. The secret is two-fold: the steak marinates in a bed of soy and lemon, and the other ingredients are smooshed into the top and bottom of the steak. The marinade/paste combination after the char-roasting, results in a kind of 'blackening,' over the coals."

3 pounds top sirloin steak, 2-inch thick

1 cup soy sauce

2 lemons, juiced

1/4 cup Worcestershire Sauce

1/2 cup Colman's Hot Dry Mustard

1/4 cup garlic powder

1/8 cup black pepper

1. Four to six hours before cooking: In a large baking dish, just big enough to hold the steak; combine the soy, lemon, and Worcestershire. Place steak in dish.

2. Sprinkle half of the powdered seasonings onto one side of the steak, and spoon some of the liquid on top of the steak to make a paste. Pierce the meat with a fork all over.

3. Turn steak over and repeat Step 2. Turn the steak every hour or so and spoon some of the liquid on top. Add more soy or lemon, if needed.

4. Let it sit at room temperature for 4 to 6 hours, loosely covered with plastic.

5. Grill for 10 to 15 minutes per side over medium-hot coals, until medium-rare.

6. Let sit for about 10 minutes on a cutting board. Slice the steak crosswise into thin slices and serve.

- Karen Everett

Serves 8 to 10

Entrées

Beef In Wine

"Nancy Bush shared this simple and delicious beef recipe from Anne McCracken. Serve over polenta, recipe below."

2 tablespoons oil

2 tablespoons butter

2 pounds stew beef, cut in bite sized pieces

1 medium onion, chopped

1 teaspoon salt

1/8 teaspoon pepper

1/2 to 1 tablespoon allspice

1 to 2 6-ounce cans tomato paste

3/4 cup red wine

2 bay leaves

1. In a large skillet, heat oil and butter until brown, add beef, onion, salt, pepper and allspice and brown.

2. Add wine and cover, simmer for a few minutes. Add tomato paste, amount depending on how much gravy you want. Add bay leaves and simmer 1 1/2 to 2 hours.

3. While meat is cooking, prepare Polenta recipe.

Polenta

1/2 cup cold water

1 1/2 cup cornmeal

1 teaspoon salt

2 1/2 cup water

4 ounces cream cheese

1. In a medium bowl, combine cold water, corn meal and salt.

2. In a saucepan over high heat, bring water to a boil. Gradually stir corn meal mixture into boiling water. Cook and stir until thick. Cover.

3. Reduce heat to low and cook 45 minutes, stirring occasionally.

4. Pour into a 9-inch pie plate. Cool 5 minutes and cut into wedges.

5. Serve each wedge topped with a 1/4 inch slab of cream cheese and then cover with the above meat.

- Nancy Bush

Serves 4

Grandma's Shepherd's Pie

"This recipe has been handed down in my family for generations. My great grandmother McQuillan immigrated to America in the late 1800's from county Antrim in Northern Ireland. It is a favorite on St. Patrick's Day. It has been updated by adding frozen vegetables to save time. May the luck of the Irish be with you!"

2 pounds russet potatoes, peeled and sliced

1 tablespoon Kosher salt

2/3 cup of half and half

4 tablespoons unsalted butter

1-1/2 cups of sauerkraut

Salt and pepper, to taste

1 tablespoon olive oil

2 pounds ground beef

1 medium yellow onion, chopped

3 cloves garlic, chopped

2 teaspoons chopped fresh rosemary

2 teaspoons chopped fresh thyme

3 tablespoons tomato paste

1 cup beef broth

3 tablespoons Worcestershire sauce

3 tablespoons flour

1 cup frozen corn

1 cup frozen peas

1 cup frozen carrots

1. Preheat oven to 400 degrees. In a medium saucepan, cover potatoes with water by ½ inch, add salt. Bring to a boil over high heat. Cook until potatoes are fork tender, 12-15 minutes. Drain and set aside.

2. In same pot over medium-low heat, combine half-and-half and butter stirring until butter is melted. Add potatoes to heated butter and half and half, in pot and combine using a masher. Stir in sauerkraut, and salt and pepper to taste. Remove from heat.

3. Meanwhile in large skillet, heat oil over medium high heat. Add beef and sauté until crumbled and no longer pink, about 6 to 8 minutes. Season with 2 teaspoons salt and 1/2 teaspoon pepper. Using a slotted spoon, transfer beef to a plate. Pour off all but 2 tablespoons beef drippings.

4. In same skillet over medium heat, cook onion until onions begin to soften, 5-6 minutes. Add garlic, rosemary, and thyme and cook, stirring, until fragrant, about 2 minutes. Return beef and accumulated juices to skillet, stir in tomato paste. Cook until paste turns dark red, 3-4 minutes. Stir in broth and Worcestershire and bring to a simmer. Sprinkle with flour and cook stirring occasionally until sauce is thickened, about 5 minutes. Stir in carrots, corn, and peas.

5. Pour beef mixture into a 13" x 9" pan and dollop mashed potatoes on top, spreading potatoes over the beef mixture. Season with a pinch of pepper.

6. Bake until beef mixture is bubbling, about 25 minutes. Remove from oven. Place a rack in upper third of oven and turn broiler on high and broil until top begins to brown, 1-2 minutes. Let cool 10 minutes before serving.

- Jackie Wittman

Serves 8

Tomato Jam

"Fabulous! Janice gave me a jar for my birthday and another for Christmas. I highly recommend making this to serve with burgers, to flavor meat loaf, spaghetti, eggs, etc." - Dawn Ashbach

5 pounds ripe Roma tomatoes, cored and finely chopped

3 cups sugar

1/2 cup lime juice

2 teaspoons salt

1/2 teaspoon ground cloves

2 teaspoons freshly grated ginger

1 teaspoon red pepper

2 teaspoons garam masala

1. In a 4 to 6 quart nonreactive heavy pot, combine first seven ingredients. Bring to a boil. Reduce heat and simmer uncovered for 1 1/2 hours or until 'jam-like' consistency. Stir occasionally to be sure no scorching on the bottom of pan. Stir in garam masala.

2. Ladle into hot sterilized half-pint canning jars, leaving 1/4 inch headspace. Wipe jar rims, adjust lids and screw bands.

3. To can, submerge jars in water bath and boil for 10 minutes. Remove jars from canner and cool on a wire rack.

- Janice DeFosse

10 half pints

Yossarian's Bolognese Meat Sauce

"Chef Yossarian came to Guemes with a long history of working in high-end restaurants. He brought all those skills to the position as the head chef at Anderson's Store. His popular Bolognese was first printed in the March 2010 Guemes Tide. Serve with pasta of your choice."

1 tablespoon olive oil

1 pound ground chuck

4 ounces pancetta (or bacon) finely diced

1/2 cup diced fresh leeks, only the white part

1/2 cup celery, diced

1/3 cup carrot, diced

1 tablespoon garlic, minced

1 cup whole milk

1/2 teaspoon ground nutmeg

1/2 teaspoon ground cinnamon

2 14-ounce cans fire roasted tomatoes, in juice

1/3 cup tomato paste

1 teaspoon freshly ground pepper

Salt, to taste

16 ounces pasta, cooked following package instructions

Parmesan or pecorino grated cheese, to serve

1. In a large thick-bottomed stock pot, over medium, heat oil and add meats until they just start to brown.

2. Add all the vegetables. Turn heat low and "sweat" the mixture, scraping the bottom of the pot with a wooden spoon (important to use wooden spoon!) until the leeks turn translucent.

3. Add everything else except pasta, salt and cheese. While stirring constantly, turn up heat to a boil.

4. Reduce heat to low simmer for 3 hours. Check on it every 10 minutes or so and stir gently. If it get too thick, add a couple more tablespoons of milk and turn simmer down lower. Cook pasta according to package directions.

5. Serve on pasta and garnish with cheese.

- Yossarian Day

Spaghetti Sauce

"For best flavor, start in the morning, bring to simmer and then let sit through the day. Or even better, make the previous day and refrigerate. This is not a definitive recipe, I make it a bit differently every time. My father's family called it macaroni gravy."

Olive oil and butter, as needed

1 large onion, diced

1 fennel bulb, diced

8 garlic cloves, minced

Olive oil and butter, as needed

1 pound brown mushrooms, sliced

1 pound lean ground beef

1 pound ground sweet sausage

Oregano, basil, thyme, fennel seed, red pepper flakes, salt and pepper, to taste

3 cans (14.5 ounces) diced tomatoes, 1 more if desired

1 jar (24 ounces) prepared tomato sauce, your taste choice

I cup freshly chopped parsley

1 teaspoon or 2 tablespoons sugar, as desired

2 cups shredded Parmesan Cheese, garnish

16 to 24 ounces bucatini pasta

1 cup pesto, or more

1. In a medium dutch oven, heat olive oil and butter, saute onion and fennel. When golden and translucent, add garlic and sauté for two minutes, do not burn. Remove from pan and set aside.

2. In same pan, heat butter and olive oil. Add sliced mushrooms in multiple batches, adding butter and olive oil, as needed. They should fry to a golden brown. (Too many at one time and they stew.) Remove from pan and set aside. (Or toss mushrooms with olive oil, salt and pepper and oven roast on a rimmed sheet pan at 375 degrees. After 15 minutes, drain liquid and continue roasting until brown, about 30 minutes more.)

3. In same pan, brown burger and sausage, again in separate batches. Meat should brown, not stew.

4. When browning meat, I season each 'fry' with the herbs, which brings out the flavor.

5. Add canned stewed tomatoes, amount varies to your liking. For thickening, add a jar of Classico tomato/basil sauce. Or! The best, "Exclusivo Wild Porcini Sauce."

6. Return onion, fennel, mushrooms to pan and heat through. (Sometimes I add oven roasted red, yellow, orange peppers.)

7. When heating sauce to serve, I like to add parsley, for a fresh look and taste. Last thing, stir in a teaspoon/tablespoon of sugar to cut the acidity and heat through.

8. Cook pasta al dente, according to package directions. Before draining, set aside 2 cups of pasta water. Toss pasta with pesto and olive oil. Add reserved pasta water, as needed, to prevent gumminess.

9. Place pasta in pasta bowls and top with Spaghetti Sauce. Serve topped with freshly grated parmesan, as desired.

- Dawn Ashbach

Serves 12

Indian Chutney

"The Everett's shared this recipe in the 1996 Evening Star. *It is excellent with pork or curries."*

2 pounds apples, peeled, cored and chopped

2 pounds brown sugar

1 quart apple cider vinegar

1 pound raisins

1 quart stewed tomatoes (32 ounces)

1 pound dates, chopped

1 1/2 pounds onion (about 3), chopped

2 tablespoons Colman's Dry Mustard

2 tablespoons ground ginger

2 tablespoons dried red peppers

2 tablespoons salt

1. In a large, heavy bottomed pot, over medium heat, cook the apples, vinegar and sugar for an hour. Stir occasionally.

2. Stir in remaining ingredients. Simmer all day until the consistency of a condiment. Pour into pint jars, cover and refrigerate.

- 'Big' Sue Everett

10 cups

Apple Chutney

"A combined Kathy Whitman and Nancy Lazara creation. It is loosely based on an Ina Garten recipe. She describes it as, 'Delicious! Zingy and gingery.' Try with meat, aged cheddar and in a Panini. There were rave reviews when we spread it on dense bread, topped with a thin apple slice from Sandy Lane's orchard."

45 ounces apples (about 12 apples, 6 cups), peeled and roughly chopped

14 ounces onions, (about 1 1/2 cups) chopped small

2 ounces (1/4 cup) minced ginger

2 whole mandarins, skin cut into eighths and chopped in a food processor

2 14-ounces cans whole cranberry sauce.

1 1/2 cups apple cider vinegar

2 1/2 cups brown sugar

1 tablespoon mustard seed

1/2 teaspoon red pepper flakes

4 1/2 teaspoons kosher salt

2 cups raisins

In a large pot, combine all ingredients except raisins. Simmer for about 45 minutes until thick and rich. Stir in raisins and remove from heat.

- Kathy Whitman

6 pints

Teriyaki Steak Korean Style

"This recipe was given to our family by a Guemes Island 'old-timer,' Dutch Propst. We recently found it in our cookbook and wanted to honor the memory of a special Guemes resident. It was obtained while Dutch was serving as a Marine corpsman in Korea in 1950. He shared it with us and we want to share it with you."

Marinade

3/4 cup soy sauce

1/4 cup water

2 teaspoon finely grated ginger, or 2 teaspoons powdered ginger

1 1/2 teaspoon brown sugar

2 teaspoons sesame seeds

1/3 cup thinly sliced green onions

1 garlic clove, minced

2 pounds sirloin tip roast

1. In a small bowl, combine all marinade ingredients.

2. Slice meat into thin strips about 1/4" to 3/8" thick. Place meat in a glass baking pan and top with marinade. Cover with plastic and refrigerate for at least 8 to 24 hours, Longer the better. Turn several times to be sure all meat is covered.

3. Broil a few minutes each side. Do not overcook!

- Mike Murphy

Serves 4

Chilaquiles Verde

"While dining at a Mexican restaurant in Gilbert, Arizona, my son-in-law ordered Chilaquiles. He let me try it and I was hooked! I dissected his plate and came up with this version. We have it for dinner every Thursday night."

Green Sauce

1 pound tomatillos, husked and rinsed (about 10 medium to large)

3 jalapeños, stemmed and seeded

1/2 medium white onion, diced

Fresh cilantro, large handful

2 cloves garlic

Juice of 1/2 lime

1/2 teaspoon cumin

Pinch of kosher salt

Toppings

1 16-ounce can black beans, drained and rinsed

1/2 cup sour cream

1/2 cup crumbled queso fresco cheese

1/2 red onion, diced

8 slices crispy fried bacon, crumbled

1 avocado, seeded, and thinly slice

5 ounces Multigrain tortilla chips

4 eggs, fried or sunny side up

1. Green Sauce: In a large saucepan or Dutch oven, combine tomatillos, jalapeños, and onions, add enough water to completely cover. Over medium high, bring to a boil. Reduce heat to low and simmer until vegetables are cooked through and soft, around 8 to 10 minutes. (Tomatillos will change color from bright to pale green).

2. Using a slotted spoon, transfer tomatillos mixture to a blender. Add cilantro, garlic, lime juice, cumin and salt, and blend until smooth. Transfer to a saucepan and keep warm under low heat.

3. Preheat oven to 200 degrees. In a 9"x9" baking dish, add chips and top with sauce. Place in oven to keep warm. Fry eggs.

4. Portion tortilla chips onto each plate. Top with equal amounts of black beans, a dollop of sour cream, followed by an egg. Garnish with queso fresca. onion, bacon and avocado.

- Patricia Bradley

Serves 4

Corn Chilies Casserole

"Dinner or brunch, this is a family favorite!"

2 cups grated cheddar cheese

1 cup fresh corn (if using frozen, allow to thaw and drain)

1 cup cooked brown rice (Basmati is my favorite)

2 7-ounce cans of diced green chilies

1 6-ounce can pimientos (or add another can of green chilis)

3 eggs

2 cups half and half

2 cups skim milk

2 tablespoons flour

1 teaspoon white pepper

1 teaspoon salt

1/4 cup grated cheddar cheese, garnish

1/2 teaspoon chopped chilies, garnish

1 4-ounce can sliced black olives, garnish

1. Preheat oven to 375 degrees. Oil a 13"x9" casserole dish.

2. Place 1 cup of cheese in bottom of dish. Evenly distribute corn, chilies and pimentos. Cover with remaining cheese.

3. In a small bowl, beat eggs until fluffy. Stir in remaining ingredients and evenly pour mixture over dish.

4. Garnish with chilies and olives, as desired.

5. Bake for 1 hour or until lightly brown.

- Kathy Whitman

Serves 8

Parmesan Crusted Chicken

"This easy and delicious dish is a Neilson family favorite. When young, our kids requested it too often! In his dating days, our son made it to impress his girlfriends. Now, our daughter makes it for her three kids often, as they love it too!"

2 eggs, well beaten

1/4 cup water

1/2 teaspoon oil

1/2 to 1 cup shredded Parmesan cheese

1 cup Progresso Italian breadcrumbs

1/2 cup butter

1 1/2 pounds boneless chicken breasts, pounded to an even thinness

1 lemon juiced

1/4 cup minced parsley

Lemon slices, garnish

1. In a small bowl, combine eggs, water and oil.

2. In another bowl, combine cheese and bread crumbs. Cover a sheet pan with wax paper.

3. Dredge prepared chicken in egg mixture and then dredge in the cheese mixture. Place chicken on wax paper, cover with another piece of wax paper and cover with a heavy sheet pan. Refrigerate a few hours.

4. Using a non-stick fry pan, over medium high, melt butter and sauté chicken quickly, turning once.

5. Sprinkle with parsley and lemon juice. Serve on warmed plates with lemon slices.

- Dianne Neilson

4 servings

Vegetables

First salmon BBQ, South Beach, August 19, 1951 at the R.O. Clippingers' beach just west of the ferry landing.

Dave's Baked Beans

"This family recipe has been handed down, in some format, for hundreds of years. The smell that fills the house as they cook....oh my! We always serve with a slaw of thinly sliced, chopped cabbage with a dressing of mayonnaise, red wine vinegar, sugar and celery seed."

2 pounds dried kidney beans

1 good sized onion, thinly sliced

1 piece salt pork, meatier the better, rinsed and rind removed

1/2 cup sugar

1/2 cup molasses, more to taste

1 heaping tablespoon dry mustard

1 teaspoon salt, more to taste

1 scant teaspoon pepper

1. In a large pot, cover beans with cold water and soak overnight.
2. In the morning, parboil beans until soft-ish and drain. Preheat oven to 400 degrees.
3. Cut salt pork in checkerboard fashion and slice in half. In the pot, layer in onion, pork and beans. Repeat, leaving some pork and onion on top.
4. In a medium bowl, combine remaining ingredients, and add to pot. Cover all with boiling water and a lid.
5. Place pot on cookie sheet covered with two layers of tin foil. Cook at 400 degrees for one hour, reduce heat to 350. Cook until done, pretty much all day.
6. Always keep beans covered with water, uncover the last 1/2 hour if liquid needs thickening. When reheating beans, additional water will be needed.

- Dave Rockwood

Serves a lot!

Onion Casserole

"Ginny Johns, a past island resident and good friend shared this recipe. When Walla Walla Sweet Onions are available, this easy casserole will be the star in a dinner menu. It is plainly delicious."

1 cup rice

1 1/2 teaspoons salt

6 tablespoons butter

2 pounds (6 to 7 cups) Walla Walla Sweet Onions, thinly sliced

1/2 teaspoon salt

1/4 teaspoon pepper

1/4 cup sour cream

1/4 cup grated Swiss cheese

1 tablespoon minced parsley

1. Preheat oven to 300 degrees. In a large pot, bring a quart of water with 1 1/2 teaspoons salt to boil. Cook the rice for five minutes, drain and set aside.

2. In a large heavy bottomed casserole pan, over medium, heat 4 tablespoons of butter. When butter foams, stir in the onions, tossing to coat well. Stir in rice and salt and pepper.

3. Cover casserole and bake for 1 hour. Remove from oven. Before serving, add sour cream, cheese, the remaining butter and parsley. Gently toss.

- Nancy Bush

Serves 6

Quinoa with Cauliflower

"Quinoa is known for its healthy attributes: lowering cholesterol, risk of diabetes and heart disease. We serve it regularly and this is one of our favorite recipes."

2 heads of cauliflower, cut into bite-size florets

Olive oil

Salt and pepper, to taste

3 cups cooked quinoa

1 large onion, chopped

1 1/2 cups pickled jalapeños, chopped

1. Preheat oven to 425 degrees. Spread cauliflower florets on a rimmed baking sheet and toss with oil, salt and pepper. Make sure to leave a little space around each floret, so they caramelize, not steam. Roast for 25-35 minutes.

2. In a large saucepan, cook quinoa, according to package directions.

3. In a large bowl, combine all ingredients. Season again with salt and pepper, to taste. Can be served hot, warm or cold.

- Gayle and Eddie Selyem

Serves 8

Vegetables/Sides

Greek Stuffed Eggplant

"Dinner at Mo and Cary Halpin's was always tasty and fun. Her friend, Ruth Denaxas, shared this Greek family recipe. It has become a favorite." - Dawn Ashbach

1 tablespoon olive oil

2 medium onions, finely chopped

1 pound lamb shoulder, coarsely ground

1 tablespoon minced garlic

1/4 teaspoon cinnamon

1 teaspoon oregano

Salt and pepper, to taste

1/2 cup pine nuts

1/2 cup bread crumbs

2 globe eggplants, peeled and cut into strips

1 to 3 tablespoons olive oil

1 16-ounce jar of good tomato sauce

1. In a large skillet, heat oil and sauté onions and garlic. Add meat and brown, drain excess oil. Add in seasoning and pine nuts and cook through. Place in bowl, toss with bread crumbs and set aside. Preheat oven to 375 degrees.

2. Slice the eggplant in 1/2 inch pieces. Place the slices on a greased baking sheet and lightly brush each with olive oil. Bake about 10 minutes, until soft. Remove from oven to cool.

3. In a greased 9"x13" baking dish, stack two rounds of eggplant together. Layer part of the filling between the two slices, like a sandwich. Top each stack with filling.

4. Pour the tomato sauce over all. And barely cover with water.

5. Bake 45 to 60 minutes, until soft.

- Mo Halpin

Serving 8

Curried Brussels Sprouts

"I have grown Brussels sprouts in my garden on Guemes Island for over 20 years. They are a fabulous and rare winter crop, because they can be harvested from December through mid-March. Even friends who don't care for Brussels sprouts have liked this easy recipe."

2 pounds Brussels sprouts, cleaned and halved lengthwise

1/2 cup mayonnaise

2 tablespoons grated Parmesan cheese

1/4 teaspoon celery seed

1/4 teaspoon curry powder

1/2 teaspoon salt

1/8 teaspoon pepper

1. In large saucepan, cover sprouts with water and steam until a fork enters them easily.
2. In separate bowl, blend together remaining ingredients.
3. Toss mayonnaise mixture with hot sprouts and serve.

- Dyvon Havens

Serves 4

Roasted Broccoli

"Roasted broccoli is a standby dish in our house. As is roasted carrots, asparagus and cauliflower. Roasting brings out the flavor and topped with lemon and parmesan, yum."

1 large head of broccoli, cut into florets

2 1/2 tablespoons olive oil

1/4 teaspoon crushed red pepper flakes

Salt and pepper, to taste

1 lemon, halved

1/4 cup freshly shaved Parmesan

1. Preheat oven to 400 degrees. In a large bowl, combine broccoli, olive oil, pepper flakes, salt and pepper.
2. Spread mixture on a rimmed baking sheet. Place lemon halves on each end of sheet, cut side up.
3. Roast, turning once until broccoli is tender crisp, about 20 minutes,
4. Remove from oven, squeeze roasted lemon over broccoli. Sprinkle with Parmesan and return to oven for 5 minutes. Can be served hot or at room temperature.

- Dawn Ashbach

Serving 4

Vegetables/Sides

Gigantes Plaki Beans

"The beans look like giant white butter beans and are known for their mild, sweet taste. These baked beans are a traditional dish in Greek cuisine. So good."

1 pound shelled dried Gigantes beans

1 teaspoon salt

1/2 cup olive oil

4 cloves garlic, chopped

1 cup chopped onion

1/2 cup chopped celery

1/4 cup chopped parsley

1 cup hot water

2 14-ounce cans of diced tomatoes

1 tablespoon dried oregano

Salt and freshly ground pepper, to taste

1. In a Dutch oven, cover the beans with water and soak overnight. In the morning, drain beans in a colander and rinse.

2. Return beans to Dutch oven, and cover beans with water, add salt and bring to a boil. Turn heat to simmer and cook for 45 minutes. Do not overcook as beans will become mushy!

3. Preheat oven to 350 degrees. While beans are cooking, spread olive oil, garlic, onion and celery on a jelly roll pan. Bake until soft, about 10 minutes.

4. Drain beans in colander, place on jelly roll pan and toss gently to coat with olive oil mixture. Add parsley, salt, pepper and hot water; blend together. Return to oven and bake 20 minutes.

5. Remove pan from oven, gently blend in tomatoes and oregano. Return to oven and bake 30 minutes or until beans are tender and sauce thickens.

6. To serve, toss in a large shallow bowl. Salt and pepper, to taste.

- Dawn Ashbach

Serves 8

Parmesan Roasted Zucchini

"Ina Garten's recipes are always so easy and so delicious." - Dawn Ashbach

6 medium zucchini, about 2 1/2 pounds

2 tablespoons olive oil

Salt and freshly ground pepper

1 tablespoon minced garlic

2 tablespoons minced fresh parsley leaves

2 tablespoons julienned fresh basil leaves

1/2 cup freshly grated Parmesan cheese

1 teaspoon salt

1/2 teaspoon pepper

3/4 cup panko

3 1/2 teaspoons olive oil

1. Preheat oven to 425 degrees. Trim the stem end of the zucchini and cut in half lengthwise. With a teaspoon, scoop out the channel of seeds.

2. Place zucchini in one layer on a sheet pan. Brush generously all over with olive oil. Turn over with the cut side down and place on sheet pan. Sprinkle with salt and pepper. (Be sure you leave space between each piece to avoid getting soggy.) Roast for 12 to 15 minutes, until just tender, but still firm when tested with the tip of a knife.

3. While zucchini is cooking, make the bread crumbs. In medium bowl, combine garlic, parsley, basil, Parmesan, salt and pepper. Add panko and olive oil; mix well.

4. Turn zucchini cut side up and spoon a heaping tablespoon of panko mixture evenly on each zucchini. Bake for another 8 to 10 minutes, until the panko is crispy. Serve hot, warm or at room temperature.

- Ina Garten

Serves 6-8

Friendsgiving Sweet Potato Casserole

"Every November, Tim and Jackie Wittman host a Friendsgiving dinner. They provide the main entrée, friends bring the sides. We have shared this take on a sweet potato pie."

Sweet Potato mixture

8 large sweet potatoes, pierced

1 cup granulated sugar

2 teaspoons salt

2 teaspoons vanilla extract

4 large eggs

1 cup butter, melted

Streusel topping

1 cup brown sugar, packed

1 cup flour

2 cups chopped pecans

1 cup melted butter

1. Preheat oven to 375 degrees. Grease a 4 quart baking pan with vegetable oil.
2. Bake potatoes until soft, about an 1 hour. Allow to cool, separate potato from skin and place in large bowl.
3. Add sugar, salt, vanilla, eggs and butter to potatoes. Using an electric beater, mix all ingredients until fluffy about 4 minutes.
4. Pour all ingredients into prepared baking pan. Bake for 25 minutes
5. Prepare streusel: In a medium bowl, combine brown sugar, flour, pecans and butter with a fork or pastry blender.
6. When potatoes are done baking, remove from oven and sprinkle with streusel topping and bake 15 minutes or until streusel is browned. Cover with foil to keep warm.

- Dawn Ashbach

Serves 16

Homemade Kraut

"The following summarizes what has been learned from the Fall of 1970 to the present. The early instructors were old time Guemes folks, Cliff Weigel, Fred Grant and George Kingston. In the 80's, another mentor was Annon May, a Tacoma lawyer of note, who had a farm by the Puyallup River."

#10 ceramic crock

Large ceramic plate

5 pound rock, sterilized

Kraut knife

Kraut tamp

Padded mat for crock

New rubberized gloves

90 pounds cabbage

26 ounces non-iodized salt

Adjuncts, as desired: Dill, onions, carrots, garlic, caraway seed, chili flakes, cayenne pepper, horseradish

1 large clean garbage bag

24 to 26 quart jars and lids

1. The two main things in making kraut (beside the cabbage) are: cleanliness; and the right amount of salt. These factors cannot be overlooked or underestimated.

2. Always sterilize all the gear. The gear : #10 ceramic crock; a plate that will fit neatly and snugly within the crock, a flat 5 pound rock; (the rock will rest atop the plate, which is used to keep the shredded cabbage below the natural moisture that will come from and be above the shredded cabbage in the crock); a kraut knife and a kraut tamp.

3. You will also need something like a padded mat to provide a cushion on which to place the crock while you are layering the shredded cabbage, and sprinkling in the salt (add other adjuncts, as you prefer---like dill, chili peppers, caraway seed, shredded carrots, garlic, onions, horseradish and the like), and tamping the shredded cabbage. The mat will reduce the chances of cracking the crock and make it easier to slide the crock into a safe position during the 3 to 5 weeks it will take for the shredded cabbage to become kraut.

4. Protection of the ceramic crock can be enhanced with a tight stainless band being affixed just below the outside upper lip on the crock. That will reduce the chances of having a plink or crack develop on the walls of the crock, while tamping.

5. You will also want a new, clean garbage sack that you can pull over the crock once the shredding, salting (and addition of any adjuncts) and tamping is done, and the plate and rock are positioned. Then put a clean cardboard box over the whole shebang and write the date when made along with whatever adjuncts/flavorings that are added. Otherwise, you will forget those details.

6. Now it is easier for me to show you how to make kraut than it is to explain.

Vegetables/Sides

Through the years my brother Dave and close island friends have helped me make kraut in late April through early June and in September, October and November. During those times you will probably find me, brother Dave, Gary Davis, Al Bush and Trish and Kelly Bradley figuring out when to pound out some more kraut, with the flavors they prefer.

7. Now, it will take about 90 pounds of cabbage to do a #10 crock; and about 24 to 26 ounces of plain salt (stay away from iodized); it's ok to use sea salt, and even pink salt, but don't use coarse salt. If you are using a #5 crock, just reduce accordingly.

8. With the cabbage, discard outer leaves or other obvious blemishes. And then start shredding the cabbage. Avoid shredding the stem or core that is way inside the cabbage. That portion might have an "off" flavor. As you shred, occasionally sprinkle in the salt, evenly distributing the salt between layers of cabbage. Evenly distributed is the idea, the layering of the cabbage with the salt and adjuncts.

9. During the shredding it will be good, once in a while, to tamp down the salted cabbage and adjuncts. This will compress the product and get rid of the air and help bring out the water that is naturally in the cabbage. It is usually not necessary to add any moisture other than what is in the cabbage. But when the crock is full of the shredded cabbage (within 3 or 4 inches of the top of the crock) you will want the plate (held down by the rock) to be under the fluid. When you are at that stage, slip the clean garbage sack over the crock; tie it on with a string and rubber band, and put the box over it, in a safe place in a garage, unheated. Then about every 4 days check to see if any "scum" is developing at the top of the plate; and if so, why just wipe it out with clean paper towels. Make sure the plate and rock keep the product weighted down.

After about 4 weeks the kraut should be done or close to done, depending on the temperature, and your tastes.

I like to "jar" the kraut in sterilized quart or pint jars at 4 or 5 weeks from the shredding. Use plastic or dentist gloves while packing the jars. Pack the jars rather tightly, and clamp down new lids and bands. Before jarring you can ladle off the excess fluid on the top of the kraut; but save it as you may want to splash some of it into the crock as you get further down into the crock, while jarring.

I like a lot of the kraut to go to friends; and keep my jars in a cold fridge for use when needed.

As said above, you can add adjuncts. I like dill with chopped onions; shredded carrots and sliced garlic can be nice. With shredded horseradish, do the shredding just before making the kraut, as the horseradish has a tendency to turn brownish rather quickly. With onions, I use Spanish and not Walla Walla Sweets, or ones like those. It's easy to toss in flakes of chili peppers. If you want to add cayenne pepper, just mix a bit of it with the salt before you start. Be conservative at first; over the years you can arrive at your favorites. And plain kraut is great. You are in control.

Pretty much you will be fine by emphasizing cleanliness and the right amount of plain salt. Not enough salt results in a lack of crispness, a mushiness, not desirable. Too much salt and you end up with salted cabbage.

And as a precaution, since the kraut knife is sharp, use a new pair of plastic or rubber covered gloves when shredding the cabbage.

This about covers the process used by my old time and departed friends. Don't be too bashful come kraut time; drop by and you might see the operation happening or find out when the next crock will be made. You can be put to work.

Cliff, Fred, George and Annon were always helpful.

- Bud Ashbach

26 quarts

Vegetables/Sides

Seaway Hollow Thanksgiving Vegetables

"The Griggs family has been on Guemes for decades and first built a log cabin at Seaway Hollow. They also built a home that was featured in Sunset Magazine *in the 1960's. Both recipes are delicious for Thanksgiving dinner and can be made ahead."*

Make Ahead Mashed Potatoes

8 large baking potatoes, peeled

1 8-ounce package cream cheese

1 cup sour cream

1 to 2 teaspoons garlic powder

1/2 teaspoon pepper

4 tablespoons butter

Paprika, dash

1. In a large pot, boil 5 quarts water, add potatoes and cook until tender, about 40 minutes. Drain and mash well with a potato ricer (do not use an electric mixer.) Return to pot.

2. In a medium bowl, beat together cream cheese and sour cream. Gradually add to potatoes and beat until smooth. Beat in garlic and pepper.

3. Turn mixture into a buttered, shallow 3-4 quart casserole. Dot with butter and sprinkle lightly with paprika.

4. Cover and chill for up to 3 days. To reheat, bring to room temperature. Preheat oven to 400 degrees. Cover and bake for 30-40 minutes.

- Donel Griggs

Serves 12-15

Gourmet Beans

"Years ago, Isabel Griggs gave me this recipe. It's a good vegetable dish if fresh beans are not available. It can be made a day ahead of serving."

2 16-ounce cans whole string beans, drained
1/2 garlic, minced
1/2 onion, sliced in 'circles'
2 teaspoons sugar
1 teaspoon paprika
1/2 teaspoon salt
1/8 teaspoon pepper
1 tablespoon oregano
2 teaspoons dry parsley
1/2 teaspoon dry mustard
4 tablespoons olive oil
5 tablespoons vinegar

In a large bowl, toss together garlic and onion. In a separate bowl, mix together remaining ingredients and pour over bean mixture. Let stand at least 1/2 to 1 hour before heating, do not boil. Cover and refrigerate if made a day ahead of serving.

- Donel Griggs

Serves 8

Justin's Nettle Pesto

"Justin's love for Guemes Island is reflected in this recipe. He had such high regard for Guemes's natural bounty, that when Edith Walden planned her visit in Atlanta, Georgia, he asked her to bring island nettles. She indeed complied and, tentatively, went through TSA inspection with 10 pounds. During her stay they perfected two recipes, Nettle Soup and Nettle Pesto. The flavors were such a hit with the family, Justin's dad ordered nettle seed to plant at their mountain home."

8 cups nettle leaves, about 1/2 pound, somewhat packed. Cut out stems and discard.

1/2 cup olive oil

1/2 cup walnuts

1/2 cup shredded Parmesan cheese

3 to 4 cloves garlic, minced

2 teaspoons lemon juice

Salt, to taste

1. In a large pot, blanch nettle leaves in 2 quarts, or more of boiling salted (1 teaspoon) water for two minutes. Using tongs, place nettles in boiling water to blanch. Drain in colander and set aside.

2. Cooked nettles will not sting. Wrap nettles in a cotton dishtowel and wring until thoroughly dry.

3. Place a packed 1/2 cup of the cooked nettles in a food processor with the remaining ingredients. Pulverize until smooth, salt to taste. Serve this Guemes Island nettle pesto, as you would any tasty pesto.

- Justin James and Edith Walden

1 1/2 cups

Seafood

George Kingston

Dungeness Crab Risotto

"In 1998, I moved to Seattle to be on the opening management team of Il Fornaio and the Risotteria in Pacific Place. The Risotteria specialized in, you guessed it, risotto! Chef Enrico Ambrosetti from Italy would make fantastic risotto all day long. It was one of the first truly authentic Italian dishes I learned to make at home and it has always been versatile to help me clean out the fridge when I have leftovers. Once you get the basic recipe down, have fun with different ingredients. I created this Guemes specific recipe for those that find themselves with some unexpected fresh crab or spot prawns given to them from generous neighbors!"

5 1/2 cups vegetable stock (or seafood stock made from shells)

2 tablespoons olive oil

3 tablespoons unsalted butter, divided

3/4 cup chopped shallot, onion or leek

1/2 cup of finely chopped fennel bulb or 2 tablespoons fresh chopped tarragon

1 teaspoon salt

3 garlic cloves, minced or pressed

1 1/3 cups Arborio rice (Italian Vialone Nano or Carnaroli)

1/2 cup dry white wine

1 pound (about 3 to 4 cups) cooked, cleaned Dungeness lump crab (body meat)

3/4 cup grated Parmesan cheese

Zest from 1 lemon

1/4 cup freshly chopped chives or parsley

Salt and pepper, to taste

1. In a large saucepan, heat stock to a simmer. Keep it hot without boiling.

2. In a heavy bottomed pot or dutch oven, over medium-low, heat oil, add 1 1/2 tablespoons butter. With a spatula, sauté aromatics (either onion, shallot or leek and fennel, if using) until softened, do not brown. Add salt and garlic and stir for 30 seconds.

3. Increase heat to medium, add rice and stir, about 3 minutes, until the rice is toasted and starts to look translucent.

4. Add wine and continue stirring for about 2 minutes, until mostly evaporated.

5. Add heated stock to rice, one cup at a time, stirring continuously until almost all of the stock is absorbed. Once you can scrape the bottom with wooden spoon and it holds without easily flowing back, repeat procedure, allowing the rice to absorb the stock after each addition. (Don't wait too long so bottom does not scorch.) When done, risotto should kind of flatten and be very creamy.

6. I recommend stirring with a wooden spoon as it helps break down the rice starch, which gives you a creamier risotto. Rice should be slightly al dente, which takes about 18 to 22 minutes.

7. When rice is done, stir in remaining butter, parmesan cheese and lemon zest. Stir, stir, stir. Season with salt and pepper, as desired.

8. When ready to serve, fold in crab and chives or parsley. (If you didn't use fennel bulb, add freshly chopped tarragon.)

9. Serve in 'pasta' bowls. If you are being fancy, top with the larger pieces of crab. Garnish with a little more chives and lemon zest, if desired.

- Travis Rosenthal

Serves 4

Dungeness Crab Panini

"We took this twist on Karen Everett's crab sandwich."

1 loaf French bread, sliced on the diagonal into 8 thick slices
1 cube butter
2 2-pound cooked Dungeness crabs, picked clean
1 pound grated cheese, cheddar or provolone
1-16 ounce bottle of chipotle chili sauce

1. Butter two slices of bread on both sides. On one slice, pile a handful of grated cheese and top with two handfuls of crab. Drizzle liberally with chipotle sauce, top with more cheese. Top with the other bread slice.

2. Heat a panini maker. When hot grill the sandwich until toasted and cheese oozes out the sides. Repeat for additional sandwiches.

- Mark and Kelly Linneman

Serves 4

Crab Cakes, Pan Fried

"It has been a journey to find the best crab cake. This one fits the bill."

1/2 cup scallions, finely minced (green part only)

3 tablespoons freshly chopped parsley (or cilantro)

1 tablespoon Old Bay Seasoning

2 large eggs, beaten

2 red bell peppers, seeded and finely diced

4 tablespoons panko or dry bread crumbs, more as needed

1/3 cup mayonnaise, more as needed

1 teaspoon salt

1 teaspoon pepper

1 pound crab meat (about 4 cups)

1/2 cup flour

5 tablespoons vegetable oil

Crab Cake Sauce

1. In a colander, drain the crab meat to remove excessive moisture.
2. In a large bowl, combine all ingredients except crab and oil. Using a spatula, gently fold in crab. Combine until mixture clings together. (If cakes are too wet to hold together, add additional mayonnaise and/or panko.)
3. Using a 1/2 measure cup, pack in crab mixture. Place each portion on a baking sheet lined with parchment paper. Press down to create 3-inch cakes.
4. Chill for at least 30 minutes; can be held for 24 hours.
5. Place flour on a plate and lightly dredge crab cakes on both sides.
6. In a large nonstick skillet, heat oil over medium high, until hot but not smoking. Gently lay crab cakes in pan and fry until outsides are crisp, about 4-5 minutes on each side. Serve with Crab Cake Sauce, if desired.

Crab Cake Sauce

1/3 cup mayonnaise

1/3 cup sour cream

1 tablespoon minced chipotle chiles (or 1 teaspoon Sriracha, more as desired)

1 garlic clove, minced

1 tablespoon horseradish

1 tablespoon minced parsley (or cilantro)

1 tablespoon lemon juice

In a small bowl, mix all ingredients. Cover and refrigerate for at least 30 minutes.

- Matt Ashbach

12 crab cakes, 1 cup sauce

Crab Rolls

"A Pacific Northwest twist on the classic East Coast Lobster Roll. A true crowd pleaser for a summer picnic. The crab mixture can be made ahead and refrigerated. Seasoning can be adjusted to your taste palate."

1 pound cooked, cleaned Dungeness crab

4 green onions, sliced

2 tablespoons chopped chives

1 cup chopped celery

2 teaspoons tarragon

1 teaspoon dill

1 teaspoon Old Bay Seasoning

Zest of one lemon

1 tablespoon lemon juice

Salt and pepper, to taste

4 split top buns, toasted

1. In a large bowl, combine all ingredients, except buns.

2. Spoon crab mixture into buns and serve. Serve with potato chips, if desired. Enjoy!

- Anne Casperson

Serves 4

Seafood

Dungeness Crab Louis

"You never know what Bud might gift you - firewood, sauerkraut, jam, berry pie, pickled beans, or crab - but you always know he arrives with a gift. When I am lucky enough to score crab, this is my go-to-recipe."

Dressing
1 cup mayonnaise

4 tablespoons chili sauce

2 tablespoons lemon juice

4 tablespoons sour cream

4 tablespoons Worcestershire Sauce

2 teaspoons Tabasco

1/4 teaspoon smoked paprika

Salt and pepper, to taste

Salad
1 large head Bibb lettuce, torn into bite size pieces

3 to 4 cups cooked, cleaned Dungeness crab

4 hard boiled eggs, sliced

6 scallions, chopped

1 cup cherry tomatoes, halved lengthwise

1 large lemon, juiced

Black olives, optional

1. To make dressing: In a medium bowl, whisk together all ingredients. Cover and set aside.

2. To assemble salad: Spread each ingredient separately on a large rimmed platter. Sprinkle lemon juice over crab.

3. Provide 4 plates so guests can build their own salad. Serve with dressing on the side.

- Tara Dowd

Serves 4

Crab Soft Tacos, Mexican Style

"My two sisters and I have been visiting Guemes for over 50 years and crabbing is a favorite family activity. I learned this recipe from a cooking teacher friend who lived in Mexico. She said it originated with Diana Kennedy. It is simple and understated. I like to serve these special tacos as an appetizer, in order to really appreciate the crab!"

4 tablespoons butter

1/2 cup finely chopped onion

1/2 cup finely chopped celery

1 tablespoon chopped mild green chiles

1 to 2 tablespoons chopped jalapeño (optional)

1 tablespoon chopped cilantro

1 to 2 cups cooked crab (1 big crab)

1 cup shredded Jack cheese

1 cup sour cream or Mexican Crema

12 corn tortillas

Cilantro, garnish

1. In a small skillet over medium, melt butter. Sauté, onion and celery until soft. Reduce heat to low, add green chilies, jalapeños (if desired), cilantro and crab. Allow to heat through. Remove from heat and cover to keep warm. Too much heat and cooked crab will get tough.

2. In a medium skillet over medium heat, warm one corn tortilla on both sides. On one side, add a tablespoon of cheese and a heaping tablespoon of warm crab mixture. Fold over and turn over to heat both sides. Repeat.

3. Top each taco with a spoonful of Crema or sour cream and sprig of cilantro.

- Nancy Lazara

Serves 6

Parmesan Baked Cod

"This is a crispy and delicious seafood entrée that is not greasy and highlights the wonderful flavor of the fish. Instead of cod, try it with boneless salmon or halibut. This recipe is sure to please any seafood lover."

4 cod fillets (about 2 pounds)

1 to 1-1/2 cups coarsely crushed pretzels

1/2 cup shredded Parmesan cheese

3 tablespoons melted butter

1 tablespoon freshly squeezed lemon juice

Salt and pepper, to taste

Fresh parsley, garnish

Lemon wedges

1. Preheat oven to 360 degrees.

2. Cut the cod fillets into 2 x 2 inch squares and arrange them in single rows on a lightly oiled glass baking dish.

3. Place pretzels in a plastic zip-lock bag and crush them "masterfully" with a wooden hammer or a rolling pin, leaving a nice mix of small, medium, and fine pieces. Do not evenly crush the pretzels to powder.

4. In a small bowl, combine the crushed pretzels, parmesan cheese, melted butter, and lemon juice and mix to a fairly rough consistency. Add salt and pepper, to taste.

5. Coat each cod fillet with the pretzel mix. It will want to roll off the sides of the fillets but keep at it.

6. Bake for approximately 25 minutes. Top fillets with fresh parsley and serve with lemon wedges.

- Tim Wittman

Serves 4

Halibut with Wasabi Pea Crust

"This recipe is from Whitewater Cooks At Home. *It has become a family favorite."*

2.5 pounds fresh halibut fillets

1 cup mayonnaise

3 tablespoons sweet chili sauce

1 1/2 cups wasabi peas, roughly chopped

1. Preheat oven to 400 degrees. Cut halibut into 6 equal pieces.
2. In a small bowl, mix mayonnaise and chili sauce together.
3. Line a baking sheet with parchment, and evenly space halibut, so they are not touching.
4. Spread the mayonnaise mixture evenly on top of each piece of halibut.
5. Top with chopped wasabi peas and firmly press onto the mayo mixture, coating the halibut.
6. Bake for 15-20 minutes, until the halibut flakes when pierced with a fork and peas start to brown slightly. Transfer to serving plates and enjoy!

- Terri Ramsay Reed

Blake's Steamer Clams

"Steamed clams are a healthy and delicious Northwest favorite. Here is a quick and easy recipe; all you need is a shovel and bucket at low tide and a handful of basic ingredients. Enjoy as an appetizer or a main course and be sure to savor the hearty broth by dipping sliced French bread."

2 tablespoons olive oil

1 medium onion, finely chopped

5 pounds Manila clams (or how many you can dig)

1 cup white wine

I bunch parsley, chopped

French bread, sliced

1. In a large skillet, heat oil over medium heat. Add onion and sauté until translucent. Add clams, wine and parsley.
2. Reduce heat to simmer, cover and steam until clam shells open.
3. Serve in pasta bowls with bread.

- Blake Marckino

Serves 4 (or one otter)

Wood Fired Steamer Clams

"Over the years, our family has enjoyed and really anticipated this delicious clam extravaganza . We cook it in our pizza oven. You can substitute an outdoor propane burner such as used to cook crab, or a large range. Serve with a hearty bread.

1 pound of bacon (thicker cut is better) cut into 1/2 inch pieces

5 pounds of Manilla or Steamer Clams, rinsed

1 bottle of Prosecco (room temperature)

5 cloves of garlic, minced

5 sprigs of fresh thyme

5 sprigs fresh oregano

1 cup of minced flat leaf or curly parsley

2 15.5-ounce cans of cannellini or great northern beans, drained and rinsed

1. In a large 24 inch skillet, (I use a cast iron Lodge skillet) over medium high heat, cook bacon until it is about 80% 'of the way you want it,' rendering the fat until bacon starts to caramelize.

2. Drain the fat as best you can, and then add the clams and about 1/2 bottle of the Prosecco to the skillet. (Drink the rest.) Sprinkle in the thyme, oregano and garlic. Cover with aluminum foil and return to heat.

3. If using a wood fired oven, it's critical to keep the flames away from the skillet, as the clams could explode. I try to keep the fire around 450 degrees and the flames indirect.

4. Use a wooden spoon to gently stir every few minutes to keep clams evenly cooked and to inspire them to open.

5. Once the vast majority of the clams have opened, add the parsley and beans.

6. Give the combination a few gentle stirs to mix in the beans and allow them to heat through. If you over stir they'll tend to fall apart and get mushy.

7. Serve in pasta bowls and enjoy with bread to sop up the delicious juice!

- Matt Ashbach

Serves 8

Salmon in Puff Pastry

"Barbecued salmon is a family favorite. This alternative is easy and impressive and can be made ahead of time and refrigerated. It can be served as main course or cut into small pieces as an appetizer. If made in advance, don't add egg wash until ready to bake."

2 tablespoons avocado oil

1 onion, diced

6 garlic cloves, chopped

Zest of one lemon

4 cups fresh baby spinach (12 ounces)

1/2 tablespoon Dijon mustard

1 8-ounce package cream cheese

1 egg, lightly beaten for wash

1 sheet frozen puff pastry, thawed in the refrigerator

1 pound fresh salmon fillets, skin removed

1. Preheat oven to 400 degrees.

2. In a large frying pan, heat oil, over medium. Sauté onion and garlic until soft, about 10 minutes. Add lemon zest and layer in spinach. When spinach has cooked down and cooled a bit, stir in mustard and cream cheese, mix well. Let cool.

3. In a small bowl, beat egg and set aside. Roll out pastry to about a 12x14-inch rectangle. Transfer pastry to a parchment lined baking sheet.

4. Spread half of the spinach mixture on one half of pastry, leaving a border. Place the salmon on top and spread the remaining spinach mixture over the salmon. To ensure a good seal, brush egg wash along edges and fold the pastry over the top and press down on edges with a fork.

5. Brush top of pastry with egg wash. With a serrated knife, score diagonally.

6. Bake for 30 minutes, pastry will be golden brown and crisp. Remove from oven and allow to rest at least 5 minutes before carving.

- Dawn Ashbach

Serves 4

Halibut in Parchment

"A delicious, easy and impressive dinner. I have made this recipe using salmon and green beans; just as tasty."

2 pounds skinned halibut, cut into 4 pieces

4 pieces of parchment paper, about 24 inches each

1 cup (8 ounces) butter, softened

1 large lemon, juiced

3 cloves garlic, minced

2 tablespoons freshly minced parsley

2 pints of cherry tomatoes (about 16 ounces), sliced in half

1 pound fresh asparagus, sliced in half

1 15.5 ounce can cannellini beans, drained (optional)

1/2 teaspoon salt

1/4 teaspoon pepper

1 tablespoon olive oil

1 sliced lemon

1. Preheat oven to 400 degrees. Pat halibut dry. Crumple the parchment paper, then 'uncrumple' and line a heavy bottomed pot or baking pan. Place each halibut piece on its own piece of parchment.

2. In a small bowl make a paste, combining butter, lemon juice, garlic and parsley. Spread on halibut fillets.

3. In a medium bowl, combine tomatoes, asparagus, cannellini beans (if desired), salt and pepper. Drizzle olive oil and toss to coat. Place vegetable mixture over halibut. Place a slice of lemon on top of each piece of halibut.

4. Fold parchment paper over and seal like a package. Place on a sheet pan and lightly cover all with aluminum foil.

5. Bake for 15-20 minutes. Remove from oven and let sit for 5 minutes. Place parchment packets on each plate.

- Dawn Ashbach

4 Servings

Easy Scallops

"This recipe can be made with sea scallops or bay scallops. There is a difference. Sea scallops are two to three times larger than bay scallops, sometimes measuring up to 2 inches in diameter. Sea scallops are not as tender but still have a sweet flavor. Either need only a short cooking time. If you want to 'gild the lily,' drizzle with a Beurre Blanc."

1 1/2 pounds fresh sea or bay scallops

1/2 cup flour

Salt and pepper, to taste

6 tablespoons butter, divided

3 large chopped shallots

1 glove garlic, minced

1/3 cup chopped parsley

1/2 cup dry white wine

Lemon, quartered and seeded

Beurre Blanc, optional, see recipe below

1. If using sea scallops, cut each in half horizontally. Dry, sprinkle with salt and pepper, toss scallops with flour. Shake off excess flour and place on a plate.

2. In a large frying pan over high heat bring 3 tablespoons of butter to a sizzle. Add scallops, in one layer, around the outside of the pan in a clockwise direction starting at 12:00, they only require a short cooking time so you want to know which ones to flip first.

3. Lower heat to medium and allow scallops to brown lightly, do not shift around. After about 2 minutes flip and cook 2 minutes more.

4. Melt the remaining butter in the pan with the scallops, add shallots, garlic and parsley. Saute together with shallots for about 2 minutes. Add wine, cook for 1 minute more. Serve with lemon.

Beurre Blanc

1/2 cup dry white wine

1/4 cup white wine vinegar

1 large shallot, chopped

1 tablespoon heavy cream

1 1/2 cubes butter

Salt and pepper, to taste

In a medium saucepan, bring wine, vinegar and shallots to a boil and reduce to a thick sauce. If you don't want it 'rustic,' strain through a fine mesh. Remove from heat and stir in cream. Whisk in butter, a bit at a time until melted. Return to heat if butter separates. You want a thick, glossy, creamy sauce. Season with salt and pepper. Hold on lowest heat, stirring occasionally, until ready to serve.

- Dawn Ashbach

Serves 4

Costa Rican Ceviche

"A tropical classic but great choice for the Pacific Northwest as well. Simple, quick, refreshing and healthy, a good choice especially on a hot summer day. Always used to make this out camping with fresh shrimp or fish. Can also use both together if desired."

2 pounds fresh raw, shelled prawns; white fish (rockfish, lingcod, cod, cabezon, halibut, snapper, mahimahi, grouper, marlin, etc.). Or combination.

2 large bell peppers, seeded and minced

3 jalapeños (less or more, as desired) seeded and minced

1 large red onion, minced

1 to 2 cups chopped fresh cilantro, as desired

12 limes, squeezed (more may be needed if small). Not bottled lime juice!

1. Slice boneless fillets into thin strips or small cubes. In a large glass or plastic bowl, combine raw prawns and/or fish.

2. Add peppers, onion, and cilantro to bowl. Slice limes and squeeze as much lime juice as necessary to thoroughly soak everything. (More is better.)

3. Thoroughly mix ingredients together. Cover and place in refrigerator to chill. Serve cold with crackers or bread.

- Nik Mardesich

Serves 4-5

Bangkok Seafood Burgers

"The original recipe was brought back from Bangkok by a friend of ours who is the owner/chef of an inn/winery in Seward, Alaska. We have amended the recipe using the availability of seafood on Guemes Island."

8 ounces well drained crab meat (about 1 cup)

4 ounces well drained shrimp (about 1/2 cup) coarsely diced

1 bunch of green onions sliced (into green for color)

1 egg white

2 tablespoons cream

2 tablespoons oyster sauce

2 tablespoons freshly minced ginger

1 teaspoon of salt

1 teaspoon of red chili flakes (finely chopped or ground)

2 cups panko

1. In a medium bowl, combine all ingredients except panko. Use your hands to make seafood burgers, size of your choice. Mixture should not be sloppy wet or falling apart. (If too wet, stir in 2 tablespoons mayonnaise or panko. More, as needed.)

2. Place panko on plate and lightly dredge burgers on both sides. Heat oven to just barely warm.

3. In a large nonstick skillet, heat oil over medium high, fry cakes about 4-5 minutes each side.

4. Put finished burgers on a cookie sheet and place in oven until ready to be served. Serve with a sauce of your choice, if desired.

- Eddie and Gayle Selyem

4-6 burgers

Classic Paella

"Typically, I make this on Labor Day, outside on large Bunsen burner. If I have a big group, I make two batches and recruit another chef to help. If available, I nestle mussels into the rice, 5 minutes after adding the shrimp. Lay the cooked crab legs on top and sprinkle with a handful of chopped red pepper and a handful of frozen peas."

1/2 cup extra virgin olive oil

1 pound Spanish chorizo, sliced into 1-inch pieces

1 pound boneless chicken, cut into 1-inch pieces

Kosher salt

1 16-ounce can diced fire roasted tomatoes

3 cloves garlic, crushed

1 tablespoon smoked paprika

2 teaspoons saffron threads

6 cups chicken broth

2 cups Bomba rice

1 pound large shrimp, peeled and deveined

If available, add:

    1 pound mussels, washed and debearded

    1 pound cooked crab legs

    1 cup chopped frozen peas

    1 cup diced red peppers

Lemon wedges, for serving

1. In a large skillet, on large burner, heat oil over medium high. Saute chorizo until browned. Remove from pan.

2. In same skillet, sauté chicken until browned. Lightly salt.

3. Move chicken to the side of skillet. Place tomatoes and garlic on the other side until tomatoes have caramelized, about 5 minutes, adjusting heat as needed. Add paprika and saffron to pan and stir to heat, about one minute.

4. Return chorizo to pan and add broth. Mix pan ingredients together and bring to a boil. Add rice and mix until rice is covered by liquid. Do not stir rice again. Cook over high heat 5 minutes then reduce heat to medium and cook 5 minutes more. Reduce heat to low, then cook 15 more minutes maintaining a gentle simmer.

5. Lightly salt shrimp, and place over rice. (If available, 5 minutes after adding shrimp, add mussels, crab, frozen peas and peppers.) Keep the paella on simmer for about 10 minutes more, until rice is mostly absorbed and al dente. When done, you will hear a crackling sound which means the rice is toasting. Poke through the middle, once rice is golden brown, remove from heat and let rest for about 5 minutes.

6. Serve on individual plates, with lemon wedges.

- Meghan Sheridan

Crab and Mushroom Casserole

"I got this recipe from Mercedes, a nurse I used to work with, the best cook I have ever met. She created many of her own recipes; the few I have from her among my favorites. Her measurements were not always precise, 'a dash of this, a large spoon of that,' so alter as desired. A great Sunday dinner during crabbing season."

4 tablespoons butter

1 1/2 cups chopped onion

2 cloves sliced garlic

1/2 pound fresh mushrooms, sliced

2 to 3 cups crab meat

1/2 cup sliced green pimento olives

1/2 cup sour cream

1 cup grated sharp cheddar cheese

1 12-ounce can whole tomatoes, quartered, including juice

1/2 teaspoon dried basil

1 1/2 teaspoon salt

1/2 to 3/4 pound (cooked al dente) spaghetti

3 tablespoons cheddar cheese, topping

1. Preheat oven to 350 degrees. In a large skillet over medium heat, melt butter and sauté onion, garlic and mushrooms.

2. Gently add remaining ingredients to pan and spread into a 9"x13" casserole. Top with additional cheese, if desired.

3. Bake for 30 to 45 minutes.

- Carolyn McCulloch

8 generous servings

Baked Salmon with Garlic Caper Sauce

"This is my favorite 'go to' sauce when I want to dress up oven-baked fish. It's easy to make and adds a delicious tangy flavor."

1/3 cup of mayonnaise

3 to 4 medium size cloves of garlic, crushed

3 tablespoons non-pareilles capers

2 tablespoons caper juice

1 1/2 pound wild salmon fillet

3 generous tablespoons of fresh lemon juice

1/4 teaspoon pepper

1. In a small mixing bowl, combine mayonnaise, crushed garlic, capers and caper juice. Stir until fully combined, cover and refrigerate for 1-2 hours for flavors to blend. This is optional; you can use it immediately if you're in a hurry.

2. Preheat oven to 350 degrees. Arrange the salmon fillet on foil lined baking sheet, skin side down. Spoon the lemon juice over the fish.

3. Spread mayonnaise mixture over entire fillet; sprinkle with pepper.

4. Bake for 10 to 11 minutes or until the edges of the salmon are opaque but inside slightly wet and translucent (thicker fillets may need more time).

5. Turn the oven temperature to broil and cook for another 2-3 minutes, browning the top of the sauce to a golden brown. Serve immediately.

- Sue Roberts

4 servings

Guemes Island Barbecue/Smoked Salmon

Win Anderson's take on the salmon barbecue, printed in the Guemes Community Club Newsletter, *1983.*

"The tradition was born in the early 1950s at R.O. Clippinger's beach (near the present Nashem house) as a PTA fundraiser. The salmon was prepared according to a procedure Bill Fast learned on Lummi Island. The event later moved to the Community Hall as a Guemes Island Improvement Club fundraiser. It was discontinued in the 1980s due to Health Department concerns."

400 pounds dressed King salmon

10 pounds rock salt

Equipment
10 pounds, 16-penny nails

1 roll baling wire

264 board feet, fir or cedar flitches

2 poles, 33 feet

6 posts, 5 feet

1 shovel

3 posthole diggers

2 five-foot pry bars

1 stack mixed dry and green alder

1 PVC pipe repair kit

1 keg Rainier

7 to 10 volunteer firefighters and/or camp followers

Day one
Assemble equipment and manpower. Combine.

Find last year's potholes to avoid rocks. Use steel pry bars because someone put the rocks back in holes last year.

When pry bar penetrates water line, send Felix for repair kit. Patch.

(Penetrating underground power line is not recommended.)

Using baling wire and nails, string poles to posts about waist height.

Fillet salmon. Nail to boards. Sprinkle with rock salt. Hose it down. Place whole mess on Arn Veal's flat bed truck and hide (11 hours). (Only the raccoons will find it.)

(For authenticity, every step in described procedure, no matter how trivial, must be accompanied by spirited debate concluded with the phrase, "I don't think we did it that way last year.")

Day two

5:15 a.m. Light fire.

The first curl of smoke wafts skyward in the flat, cool morning air as the 33-foot-long kindling row is touched off. There is no debate. No good natured "friendly advice," no discussion. That's because no one but Dave Rogers would be up at this hour and one suspects he camped in the pump house.)

7 a.m. Add green alder to fire.

This serves to produce the smoke that makes the keg of beer a medical necessity required by the local fire-safety agency. This year at 7:30, Al Bush announced he was on his third glass of foam and was "about to give up work." With further treatment, however, he pulled through.

8:59 a.m. Put fish on boards vertically. Base of the boards should be about 8 inches from the fire that is more coals than flame.

The salmon should be constantly turned end for end. When tested, the salmon will lose approximately one-third of its weight during the ordeal, according to scientific tests.

The keg will lose approximately 90 per cent of its weight, according to tests performed by Lon Schofield. No tests were performed on the firefighters.

Cook for three to five hours and serve.

- Win Anderson.

Serves approximately 600

Seafood

Spicy Asian Black Cod

"This is one of our house favorites, it never disappoints, especially if you love buttery dense fish with an Asian flavor influence. You don't have to make it spicy, I'm sure it would still delight the senses. Serve with a vegetable and rice. I started making it for my husband when I moved to Guemes Island in 2022. It is part of our delicious, new journey together."

Marinade

1/4 cup rice vinegar

1/4 cup soy or tamari

1 tablespoon brown sugar (if tamari, don't use sugar)

1 teaspoon garlic powder

1 tablespoon sambal oelek (use more, as desired.)

1/2 teaspoon cayenne

In a small bowl, combine all ingredients. Cover and set aside. Prepare 30 minutes before using, but overnight is better.

Fish

1 tablespoon olive oil

8 ounces Black Cod (Sable Fish)

1. Place marinade in a small saucepan, and reduce by half over medium heat.
2. Turn on broiler. Coat broiler pan with oil. While cooking fish, Place fish on pan, How long you broil the fish, depends on the density. Thinner fillets will cook in just 6 minutes; a thicker piece will take longer, up to 10 minutes. Fish is done when it flakes easily when pierced with a fork.
3. Plate and top with the reduced marinade, as desired.

- Dawn Omey

2 servings

Soups

School Picnic, 1926 or 1927

Basic Soup Recipe

"An easy and nutritious recipe you can make your own, using veggies on hand. The Carrot Ginger is a Lynne Myall favorite. The recipe is portioned for 2, but easily multiplied."

4 tablespoons butter

2 tablespoons chopped celery

2 tablespoons chopped onion

4 teaspoons all-purpose flour

1/2 teaspoon instant chicken bouillon granules

Salt and pepper, to taste

2 cups whole milk

Dash of Worcestershire sauce

1 cup cooked vegetables (such as carrot, cauliflower, broccoli, or potato)

1. In a heavy saucepan, melt butter and sauté celery and onion. Stir in flour, bouillon, salt, and pepper until blended. Add milk and Worcestershire sauce all at once. Stir until thickened and bubbly, then cook and stir for 1 minute more.

2. Cool slightly. Add vegetables and blend with an immersion blender, or carefully place in a blender and cover. Blend for 30 seconds or until smooth. Return to the saucepan, add variations of your choice and heat through.

Possible variations:

Carrot-Ginger: To the base, add 1 cup cooked carrots and 1/2 teaspoon curry powder and blend. Garnish with chopped peanuts and or sliced green onion. Nutmeg, cumin or cinnamon are also good additions.

Curry-Cauliflower: To the base, add 1 cup cooked cauliflower, and 1/2 teaspoon curry powder and blend. Garnish with sliced green onion and/or chopped cilantro. Curry flavor also pairs well with potato, parsnip or butternut squash.

Broccoli-Cheese: To the base, add 1 cup cooked broccoli, add 2 tablespoons grated cheddar and dash of garlic salt and blend. Garnish with additional cheese. Potato and cauliflower variations work well with cheese, as well.

Creamy mushroom with chives: To base, add 1 cup cooked sliced mushrooms. Garnish with chives, fresh thyme or a scattering of briny capers.

Dilled potato: To base, add 1 cup cooked potatoes and 1/4 teaspoon dried dill weed and blend. Carrot, sweet potato and spinach also pair nicely with dill.

Creamy spinach and tarragon: To base, add 1 cup cooked spinach, and 1/4 teaspoon dried crushed tarragon.

- Toni Schmokel and Sharon Hughlitt

Serves 2

Lemon Chicken Orzo Soup

"When you make soup weekly for around 60 people, you are always looking for something new. This one caught our eye. As a variation you could add feta, spinach or sausage. It is light and healthy, and comforting. Great any time of year."

4 sticks celery, chopped

2 carrots, chopped

1 medium onion, chopped

2 tablespoons olive oil

4 garlic cloves, minced

2 tablespoons flour

6 cups low sodium chicken broth

1 teaspoon Italian seasoning

1 1/2 to 2 pounds uncooked chicken breasts, cut into 1-inch pieces

1 cup uncooked orzo

1 tablespoon lemon juice

2 tablespoons chopped fresh parsley

Salt and Pepper, to taste.

1. In a large pot, over medium heat, sauté celery, carrots, and onion with olive oil over for 5 to 7 minutes. Add garlic and cook for about 30 seconds, then add the flour and cook for another minute or so, dissolving the flour as much as possible.

2. Add chicken broth and stir until the flour has completely dissolved. Add the chicken and Italian seasoning. Bring to a boil, then partially cover and turn down the heat. Simmer for 15 minutes.

3. Stir in the orzo and cook for another 10 minutes or until the orzo is cooked through, stirring frequently so the orzo doesn't stick to the bottom.

4. When orzo is done, add lemon juice, parsley and season the soup with salt and pepper as needed. Serve immediately.

- Beverly James and Deanne Savage

12 servings

West African Peanut Soup

"This recipe was adapted from the, 'Sundays at Moosewood Restaurant' cookbook. It is a favorite go-to on a cold day. The sweetness will depend on the carrots and yams/potatoes . When you taste the soup, you may want to add a bit of sugar to enhance the flavors."

1 tablespoon peanut or vegetable oil

2 cups chopped onion

1/2 teaspoon Sriracha sauce

1 teaspoon (or more) fresh peeled and grated ginger root

1 cup chopped carrots

2 cups chopped sweet potatoes or yams

4 cups vegetable or chicken stock

1/2 cup orange juice

1 cup peanut butter

1 tablespoon sugar (optional)

1 cup chopped scallions or chives, for topping

1. In a large soup pot, heat oil and sauté the onions until just translucent. Stir in the fresh ginger and carrots, and sauté a few more minutes.

2. Mix in the potatoes, stock, and Sriracha. Bring to a boil and simmer for about 15 minutes or more until the vegetables are tender. Let cool.

3. When cool, purée the vegetable mixture in a food processor or with an emulsifier. Add orange juice and puree again.

4. Return the purée to the pot and stir in the peanut butter and optional sugar until smooth. Reheat the soup gently, do not scorch. Add additional stock if needed. Serve warm topped with scallions or chives, if desired.

- Marietta Harrigan

Serves 6-8

Vegetable Tom-Yum Soup

"This traditional soup is popular in all Thai homes. This version, from my mother, is my favorite. If you would like, add cooked meat after the vegetables (step 7). You may know me, as I am your part-time mail delivery person."

1 red bell pepper, seeded and chopped

1 green bell pepper, seeded and chopped

1 red onion, chopped

1 cup cherry tomatoes, sliced in half

3/4 cup shimeji mushrooms

1 14-ounce can baby corn

2 sticks lemongrass, peeled and ends smashed

1 medium piece galangal, roughly chopped

1 Thai red chili pepper

6 lime leaves, torn

2 tablespoons coconut oil

1/4 cup red Thai curry paste

1/2 cup coconut milk

3 liters water (about 12 3/4 cups) (about 3 quarts)

5 tablespoons soy sauce

2 tablespoons maple butter

2 tablespoons tamarind paste

2 limes, juiced

Garnish

 Green onion, freshly chopped

 Cilantro, freshly chopped

Lime wedges

1. In a large bowl, combine bell peppers, onion, tomatoes, mushrooms and corn and set aside. In another bowl, place lemon grass, galangal, chili pepper and lime leaves and set aside.

2. In a stock pot, over medium, heat the coconut oil and curry paste. When the paste begins to sizzle, stir for about 4 to 5 minutes. If it starts to look dry, add 2 to 3 tablespoons of the coconut milk.

3. When the paste looks very soft with a deep red color and most of the liquid is evaporated, stir in the coconut milk.

4. To the pot, add water, and reserved lemongrass, galangal, chili pepper and lime leaves.

5. Cover the pot and bring to a boil. Then, turn to medium-low and simmer uncovered for 10-15 minutes.

6. Remove the solid ingredients from broth (keep them in, up to you).

7. Add reserved bell peppers, red onion, tomatoes, mushrooms and corn to the broth.

Soups

8. Add the soy sauce, maple butter, tamarind paste and lime juice.

9. Give the pot a good stir and turn the heat to medium high. Once it comes to a boil, it's ready to serve.

10. Top soup with green onions, cilantro, and serve with lime wedges.

- Sutheera Marshall (Tuptim Su)

6-8 servings

Chicken Curry Soup

"This soup was a favorite of my 'kids' (now in their 40's) when they were growing up. Now it is the most requested dinner by my grandkids when they come to GG's house at Kelly's Point."

1 medium onion, diced

2 medium carrots, diced

2 to 3 tablespoons curry, as desired

6 cups chicken broth

2 whole chicken breasts, each cut into 3 pieces each

1/2 cup jasmine rice

2/3 cup half and half

Salt and pepper, to taste

'I use a Cuisinart food processor to prepare onions and carrots.'

1. In a soup pot over medium heat, sauté onion and carrots until softened, about 8 minutes. Stir in curry, add chicken broth and bring to a boil.

2. Add chicken breasts and rice, simmer for about 20 minutes, until rice and breasts are cooked.

3. Using a slotted spoon, remove chicken from soup and place in the food processor. Process until just shredded and return to soup.

4. Stir in half and half, heat through. Add salt and pepper.

- Terri Gaffney

Serves 8

Irish Potato Leek Soup

"This creamy Irish soup is especially tasty because of the dill seasoning. It is a favorite with the 'Soup to Go' folks. They serve it with Lorraine Francis' Beer Bread and Crispy Lemon Cookies, included in this book. Include these recipes in your St. Patrick's Day menu."

2 teaspoons butter

2 cups leeks, chopped

2 stalks celery, diced

1 small onion, diced

2 cloves garlic, minced

4 cups chicken stock

4 medium potatoes, coarsely chopped

1/2 teaspoon ground black pepper

1/2 teaspoon dried basil

1 1/2 cups whole milk

2 teaspoons fresh parsley, chopped

2 teaspoons fresh dill, chopped

2 teaspoons fresh tarragon, chopped

1. In a large pan, melt the butter and add the leeks, celery, onion and garlic.

2. Saute over medium heat, until the vegetables are soft.

3. Stir in the chicken stock, potatoes, pepper, and basil. Bring to a boil.

4. Simmer over medium heat for 20 to 30 minutes, until the potatoes are easily pierced with a fork.

5. Add the milk and herbs, return to a light simmer, stirring occasionally.

6. Remove the soup from the heat and let sit for about 5 minutes.

- Julie Pingree and Joyce Fleming

Serves 6

Portuguese Clam Chowder

"During my time at the Port of Anacortes, I was often invited down to the boats for lunch. The best clam chowder I have ever tasted was on a Crowley tugboat. It was prepared by the tug captain and always a favorite according to the crew. It was his wife's grandmother's recipe from Portugal. It makes a lot, so invite friends."

5 7-ounce cans or 1 big Costco can of chopped clams

7 strips of bacon

1 quart and 1 cup 2 percent milk

1 cube butter, or 4 tablespoons butter and 4 tablespoons olive oil

1 cup flour

3 stalks celery, diced

3 carrots, diced

3 medium potatoes, cut in 1-inch pieces

1 large onion, finely chopped

4 cloves, minced garlic

1 teaspoon Johnny's Seasoning Salt

1/4 teaspoon cayenne pepper

6 to 7 drops Tabasco sauce

1/4 teaspoon dried thyme

1/4 teaspoon dried basil

1/4 teaspoon dried dill

1/2 teaspoon black pepper

1 tablespoon chopped parsley

Salt and pepper, to taste

1/2 cup white wine, if desired

1. In a large pot, combine carrots, celery and potatoes in pot with enough water to cover and boil until just tender. Don't cook too long or will turn to mush. Retain 1/2 cup stock/water, drain vegetables and set aside.

2. In same pot, cook bacon until crisp. Remove from pot and set aside. Chop when cool.

3. Drain bacon fat, keeping about 2 tablespoons in pot and cook onion and garlic until transparent. Remove from pot and set aside.

4. To make roux, in same pot, add butter, and flour. Slowly add milk, stirring constantly. It will become very thick.

5. To the roux, add vegetables and the 1/2 cup stock/water. Add clams and 'liquor,' stirring constantly. Add the rest of the seasonings, bacon and parsley.

6. Turn down heat and simmer 20 minutes; keep stirring. "I use one of those heat resistant spatulas, to keep the bottom of the pot scoured clean, as not to burn. Salt and pepper to taste. Add wine, if desired, and heat through."

- Mike Hardy

Serves 10

Roasted Butternut Squash Soup

"This a very popular soup at the Holiday Bazaar, we use: 21 pounds squash, 12 apples, 6 to 8 onions, 6 quarts vegetable broth, 3 teaspoons curry powder. I have cut down the proportions for family use."

3 to 4 pounds butternut squash, peeled and seeded

2 yellow onions

2 apples, peeled and cored, McIntosh or Golden Delicious

3 tablespoons olive oil

Salt and pepper, to taste

2 to 4 cups vegetable stock

1/2 teaspoon curry powder

Salt and pepper, to taste

1. Preheat oven to 425 degrees. Cut the squash, onions and apples in 1-inch cubes. Place on a sheet pan and toss with oil, salt and pepper. Divide the mixture between 2 sheet pans and spread in a single layer. Roast for 35 to 45 minutes, until tender.

2. While squash mixture is baking, in a medium pot, heat stock to simmer.

3. When vegetables are done, put through a food mill fitted with the medium blade.

4. Place processed vegetables in a large pot, add curry powder. Stir in enough stock to make a thick soup and heat through. Salt and pepper, to taste.

- Lorraine Francis

6-8 servings

Butternut Squash, Kale and Ham Soup

"This is a favorite Stapp family recipe. Perfect fare to share, with warm crusty bread, on rainy, blustery day."

1 medium butternut squash, cut into 1-inch chunks

1 medium onion, finely chopped

2 cups carrots, coarsely chopped

2 cups celery, coarsely chopped

2 cloves garlic, chopped

Olive oil, butter, as desired

1 20-ounce can of hominy, rinsed and drained

1 quart chicken broth

2 cups chopped ham, more as desired

1 large bunch fresh kale, chopped

1. In a large pot, steam or simmer squash until tender. Drain, and return to pot.

2. While squash is simmering, in a large frying pan, over medium high, heat oil and butter, sauté onion, carrots, celery and garlic until soft.

3. Add sautéed vegetables, hominy, chicken broth, ham and kale to the pot.

4. Allow to simmer until heated through and kale is limp. Add more broth, as desired. Salt and pepper, to taste.

- Sue Stapp O'Donnell

6 Servings

Karen Everett's Award-Winning Chili

"During the 1980's I worked at Duke's Restaurant on Queen Anne Hill in Seattle. I have modified my "Duke's-Style-Chili" over the years. In 2010, this recipe placed first in the Super Bowl Chili Cook-Off at the Brown Lantern in Anacortes."

1/4 pound ground beef (use more if you like it more meaty)
1/4 pound country pork sausage
5 garlic cloves, minced
1 medium yellow onion, chopped
1/2 green bell pepper, chopped
1/2 red bell pepper, chopped
2 tablespoons Italian herb seasoning, to taste
1/2 tablespoon chili powder, to taste
1 teaspoon garlic salt, or regular salt
1 tablespoon cumin, to taste
1 15-ounce can red kidney beans
1 15-ounce can cannellini (white kidney) beans
1 15-ounce can black beans
1 15-ounce can seasoned chili (pinto) beans
1 28-ounce can Italian diced tomatoes
1 15-ounce can fire roasted corn, if desired
1/4 cup sriracha hot chili sauce, to taste
2 tablespoons brown sugar, to taste
1 to 2 tablespoons ground cumin, to taste
1 tablespoon black pepper

1. In a large stockpot on medium heat, place meats and garlic, sprinkle with half of the seasonings. Brown, stir, layer with remaining seasonings. Break up the meats with wooden spoon.

2. Add onion and peppers. Stir and cook some more.

3. Add beans, tomatoes and brown sugar and stir. Simmer for about 2 hours, stirring occasionally.

4. Adjust seasoning with more or less of the sugar, sriracha, cumin and pepper.

5. If chili sits overnight, add water to bring it back to desired consistency (not too thick).

6. Serve each bowl topped with freshly chopped cilantro, shredded cheddar, chopped onion and sour cream.

- Karen Everett

Serves 8

White Chili

"I have served this chili to friends at Horse Nights. It tastes great in a sourdough bread bowl topped with grated Monterey Jack cheese, keeping with the white theme."

1 tablespoon vegetable oil

1 medium onion, diced

1 1/2 teaspoon garlic powder

1 pound chicken breast, sliced into 1/2 inch pieces

2 15.5-ounce cans great northern beans, drained and rinsed

2 cups chicken broth

2 4-ounce cans chopped green chilies

1 teaspoon red pepper flakes, more as desired

1 teaspoon salt

1 teaspoon cumin

1 teaspoon dried oregano

1/2 teaspoon pepper

1 cup sour cream

1/2 cup heavy cream

1 teaspoon sriracha sauce, or more

1. In a large skillet, over medium heat oil and saute onion and garlic powder together, until onion is soft. Add chicken and saute until cooked through.

2. Add to the skillet: beans, broth, chilies and seasonings. Bring to a boil.

3. Reduce heat; add sour cream, heavy cream and sriracha. Heat through and enjoy.

- Renee Norrie

Serves 6

Quinoa Chili, Vegan and Gluten Free

"The size of the diced veggies and the length they are cooked impacts whether this feels very 'veg forward' or not. The longer they cook, the more the veggies break down, the more the recipe feels like a traditional chili. (Check to see if canned beans and chocolate are vegan as sometimes they are not.) The chili can be eaten the same day although I think the flavors are deeper the next day."

2 tablespoons vegetable oil

1 large onion, diced

1 celery stalk, diced

2 large bell peppers (red and green) seeded and diced

3 cloves garlic, minced

2 teaspoons ground cumin

1 tablespoon chili powder

2 teaspoons ground cinnamon

1 teaspoon red pepper flakes, more as desired

1/2 teaspoon salt

1 cup uncooked organic quinoa

2 28-ounce cans organic diced tomatoes, in juice

2 15-ounce cans organic beans (black and pinto) including liquid

1 cup vegetable broth, more as needed for consistency

2-3 ounces of a good quality dark chocolate, roughly chopped

Salt and pepper, to taste

1. In a large pot, over medium/medium-low heat oil, sauté onion, celery, peppers, garlic until soft. Lower heat if vegetables begin to brown. Add spices and salt, stir to blend and sauté a bit longer.

2. Add quinoa, tomatoes, and beans plus liquid.

3. Simmer, on low, until quinoa is cooked, about 20-30 minutes. Stir often to keep from scorching. Blend in broth and heat through. Add more broth, if need for desired consistency.

4. Stir in chocolate, to melt and blend. Add salt and pepper, to taste.

- Lisa Kennan-Meyer

Serves 4

Winter Chicken Soup

"The fennel and escarole add unique flavor to a traditional chicken soup. Delicious on a cold winter day."

1 whole chicken breast

1 teaspoon salt

1 tablespoon olive oil

1 cup chopped onion

1 bulb fennel, trimmed, cored, and chopped

5 medium carrots, peeled and sliced

4 cloves garlic, minced

1 1/2 teaspoons dried thyme

1 teaspoon dried fennel

8 cups chicken broth

2 cups dried orecchiette pasta

2 15-ounce cans cannellini beans, rinsed

1 small head escarole, roughly chopped (about 4 cups)

Salt and pepper, to taste

Fennel fronds, garnish

1 cup Parmesan cheese

1. In a medium stock pot, place chicken breast, cover with water (about 4 cups) add salt and bring to a boil. Reduce heat, cover and simmer until done, about 15 minutes. Remove chicken from broth to cool, cut into bite-size pieces. Reserve broth in pot.

2. In a large frying pan, heat oil over medium heat. Sauté onion, fennel, carrots, and garlic until tender. Stir in dried herbs, heat and set aside.

3. In stock pot, add chicken broth to reserved broth and heat to boiling. Cook pasta, al dente, according to package directions.

4. Add vegetable mixture, beans, chicken and escarole to pasta and heat through. Avoid overcooking as pasta should remain firm. Salt and pepper, to taste.

5. Garnish with leafy fennel fronds. Serve with Parmesan cheese.

- Dawn Ashbach

8 servings

Allen Moe's Minestrone

"I have been making this recipe for years and as a result everyone thinks I'm a great cook. But really, it is the only recipe I know and it is super good for you. Because of the delicacy of the flavors, follow the directions exactly. You can add chopped up chicken for those who think they might starve otherwise."

1/2 cup olive oil

2 large onions, diced

4 to 6 garlic cloves, chopped

2 to 4 carrots, peeled and chopped

3 large celery stalks, chopped

1 1/2 teaspoon salt, divided

4 to 5 kale leaves, chopped

1 medium cabbage, cored and chopped

1/2 teaspoon thyme

2 bay leaves

3 quarts water or chicken broth

1 28-ounce can plum tomatoes, quartered, including juice

1 16-ounce can garbanzo beans, including liquid

1 cup small pasta shells

Salt and pepper, to taste

1. In a large heavy bottomed pot over low, heat olive oil and sauté onions, garlic, carrots, celery and 1/2 teaspoon salt, until onions are wilted.

2. Add cabbage, kale, thyme, bay leaves and the remaining 1 teaspoon salt. Increase heat and cook 1 to 2 minutes, stirring constantly.

3. Add water (or broth), tomatoes and garbanzo beans; bring to a boil. Lower heat and simmer, covered, for 45 minutes. Add pasta and cook 15 minutes more. Salt and pepper, to taste.

- Allen Moe

Serves 6

Gazpacho

"This cold soup, made ahead, is perfect for a hot, summer party. I served it at a horse get-together, and it was a huge hit."

6 Roma tomatoes, two fire roasted

1 English cucumber, peeled, seeded and diced

1/2 red onion, diced

1/2 red pepper, seeded and diced

1/2 yellow pepper, seeded and diced

1 jalapeno, seeded and diced

2 celery sticks, diced

1 lemon, juiced

1 teaspoon red wine vinegar

2 tablespoons olive oil

3 garlic cloves, minced

1/4 teaspoon cayenne, more as desired

1 teaspoon salt

1/4 teaspoon pepper

24-ounce bottle spicy V8 juice

Sour cream, if desired

Shrimp, if desired

1. Place all ingredients in a large blender. Mix until soup is at your desired consistency.

2. Cover and chill for two hours or overnight.

3. Pour into serving bowls and top as desired.

- Janice DeFosse

Serves 10

Iversen Gazpacho

"Jan Iversen's home on South Beach has a restaurant style kitchen, where she cooks up and serves meals for friends. This is a summer favorite."

1 quart Clamato juice
1/2 cup diced cucumber
1 avocado, diced
1/4 cup finely diced sweet onion or shallots
1/2 cup diced green pepper
1/2 cup diced celery
1/2 cup salad shrimp
2 tablespoons olive oil
3 tablespoons red wine vinegar
Pinch of sugar
1 grated garlic clove
1/2 teaspoon Cajun seafood seasoning
3 to 4 shakes of Cholula hot sauce, to taste
Salt and pepper, to taste
Cilantro leaves, for garnish

In a large bowl, combine all ingredients and chill. Add more hot sauce, to taste.

- Jan Iversen

Serves 6

Angela's Hearty Winter Soup

"When I moved to Guemes Island, I had a lot to get the hang of, including living off-the-grid in the woods. During that first cold winter, I discovered the joy and comfort of a steaming bowl of hearty soup. Not only did it provide the nourishment and energy I needed, it soothed my soul and lifted my spirits."

1 tablespoon extra virgin olive oil

1/2 red onion, diced

1 large carrot, chopped

2 stalks celery, chopped

1 turnip, chopped

2 cloves of garlic, minced

1 teaspoon marjoram

1 teaspoon basil

1 teaspoon oregano

Salt and pepper, to taste

1 14-ounce can kidney beans, drained and rinsed

1 28-ounce can diced tomatoes

1 cup green beans

2 cups chopped kale

1 cup uncooked brown rice

6 cups vegetable or chicken stock

Parmesan, grated

1. In a large pot, heat olive oil over medium-low heat until it's hot but not smoking.

2. Add onions, carrots, celery, and turnip; stir regularly until vegetables have softened.

3. Add garlic, herbs, salt and pepper. Stir for one minute until the mixture becomes steamy and fragrant

4. Add kidney beans, tomatoes, green beans, kale, rice, and broth. Stir to combine. Heat to boiling, then immediately reduce heat to medium-low.

5. Simmer soup with lid tilted over the pot until vegetables and rice are tender. Stir every twenty minutes. Taste soup each time you stir it. Adjust seasoning as needed.

6. When the vegetables and rice are cooked through, your soup is done. Serve with Parmesan cheese.

- Angela Starston

6 Servings

Asian-Style Soup

"I'm not sure of the historical implications of this recipe, but it has been a favorite of mine for (gasp) some fifty years. Maybe having to do with growing up on the west coast with Japanese-American farm families. Also my long association with serrano chilies."

3 to 4 tablespoons toasted sesame oil, enough to lightly cover the bottom of the pan.

5 or more large garlic cloves, finely chopped

2 to 4 Serrano (green) chilis, finely chopped

2 heaping tablespoons finely chopped ginger root

20 large fresh prawns, peeled (approximately one pound)

2 quarts water, or a little more

1/2 cup red miso

4 limes, juiced

1 Napa cabbage, sliced across the leaves to produce linguini-like strands

2 packages Japanese-style Somen noodles (the kind that take one minute or so to cook. Angel hair pasta can be substituted

6 tablespoons soy sauce, or more to taste

1 avocado, cut into 1/2-inch chunks and tossed with lime or lemon juice.

One bunch of cilantro, chopped

1. In a large fry pan, over low, heat oil. Sauté garlic, chiles and ginger roots.

2. Add the prawns and sauté until opaque (maybe three or four minutes). Remove from the pot and set aside.

3. Add the water and bring to a boil, adding the red miso and stirring. Add the lime juice (four limes). Taste and adjust for salt using the soy sauce. (I'm not averse to adding a glass of dry white wine.)

4. Add the noodles and cook for one minute (or more if using spaghetti), then add the cabbage. Turn off the heat and stir.

5. Serve soup in bowls. Add five prawns to each bowl. Garnish each bowl with chopped avocado and the cilantro.

- Syd Stapleton

4 servings

Justin's Nettle Soup

"Late March, early April is nettle harvest time. Use gloves when collecting the young shoots or the tender tops. (The leaves get tough after the plants blossom.) This recipe was originally posted in the April 2014 Guemes Tide."

10 cups nettle leaves, about 1/2 pound, somewhat packed. Cut out stems and discard.

1 tablespoon olive oil

1 large sweet onion, diced

1 1/2 pounds diced potatoes, about 4 cups

6 cups broth, vegetable, chicken or blanching water

3/4 teaspoon ground pepper

3/8 teaspoon nutmeg

1/2 cup half-and-half

Salt, to taste

1. In a large pot, blanch nettle leaves in 2 quarts, or more of boiling salted (1 teaspoon) water for two minutes. Using tongs, place nettles in boiling water to blanch. Drain in colander and set aside.

2. In the same pot, heat oil over medium heat, add onions and cook until they soften. Add potatoes, stock and seasoning. Bring to a boil and cook for 15 minutes.

3. Using an immersion blender, finely blend the potatoes, onions and stock. Add blanched nettle leaves (about 1 cup or more, to taste) and blend until everything is thoroughly mixed and smooth. Blend in half-and-half. Add salt and pepper, to taste. Soup may be served cold or hot.

- Justin James and Edith Walden

4-6 Servings

Breakfasts

Fourth of July 1943, North Beach

Walnut Blueberry Oatmeal Pancakes

"My husband's fraternity brother, George Sybrant, was the head chef for the Seattle Seahawks football team. He said this was a great hit at training camp. Serve hot with butter and blueberry syrup."

1 1/2 cup quick cooking oats

1 cup plain yogurt

2 1/2 cups milk

1 1/2 tablespoons honey

3/4 cup biscuit mix

1 teaspoon baking soda

3 large eggs, beaten

1/2 cup chopped walnuts

1/2 cup blueberries

1 tablespoon oil

1. In a large bowl, combine first 6 ingredients. Mix in eggs. Add additional milk, as needed to thin batter.

2. Heat skillet over medium heat. Coat pan with oil. Spoon batter into skillet, the size of pancake you want, and sprinkle with walnuts and blueberries. Cook until brown on both sides.

- Nancy Bush

4 servings

Skagit Valley Dutch Baby

"Skagit Valley offers an amazing variety of seasonal fruits. Top this yummy Dutch Baby with plain yogurt and your choice of blueberries, blackberries, raspberries, tayberries, or apricots, peach preserves or marmalades. The yummy traditional topping of butter, lemon, and powdered sugar, also works."

4 tablespoons butter

4 large eggs, room temperature

1/2 cup whole milk

1/2 cup flour

2 tablespoons granulated sugar

1 teaspoon nutmeg

1 teaspoon vanilla

1/4 teaspoon salt

1 cup of fruit, as desired

Confectioners sugar, for dusting

1. Preheat oven to 425 degrees. Place 10-inch cast iron pan in oven, melting butter.
2. In a medium bowl, combine eggs, milk, flour, sugar, nutmeg, vanilla, and salt. Pour into heated cast iron pan.
3. Bake at 425 degrees for 20 minutes, until puffy and golden. Reduce temperature to 300 degrees, and bake 5 minutes.
4. Remove from oven and rest 10 minutes. Cut into wedges and serve with above suggestions.

- Pat Richley-Erikson

Serves 8

Helen Trefethen's Genuine Swedish Pancakes

"Helen learned the recipe from a friend from Europe. Our whole family loved them plain with maple syrup. A vegan version can also be made by substituting the milk, eggs and butter with oat milk, or any preferred plant milk, egg replacer (such as Bob's Red Mill Egg Replacer), and vegan butter or an oil of your choice."

Full Batch: 9 pancakes

3 eggs

1 cup of milk

1 cup of flour

1 tablespoon butter

Small batch: 5 pancakes

2 eggs

1/2 cup of milk

1/2 cup of flour

1 tablespoon butter

1. In a medium bowl, combine first three ingredients, don't over mix.
2. In a medium frying pan, melt butter.
3. Pour a little of the mixture into the pan and move the pan around so that it covers the entire pan.
4. When the edges start to come up, flip it over. It will be done quickly after flipping. Repeat with remaining mixture.
5. Serve with maple syrup or toppings of your choice.

- Laurie Scott and Tyler Clausen

5 to 9 pancakes

Spinach Frittata

"It is easy to alter the recipe according to ingredients you have on hand."

1-2 tablespoons butter

1 large onion, chopped

1 garlic clove, minced

16 ounces spinach, stems removed

Cooked protein of your choice

6 ounces crumbled Feta Cheese, more as desired

4-6 large eggs, room temperature

1/4 cup water

Salt and pepper, to taste

2 tablespoons crumbled feta cheese, garnish

1. Preheat oven to 400 degrees.
2. In a large, oven-safe skillet melt butter. Sauté onions and garlic until soft, about 3 minutes. Layer spinach over onion and garlic.
3. Crumble protein (crab, salmon, tofu, chicken, ham) on top of spinach. Sprinkle feta over the protein layer.
4. In a medium bowl, whisk together eggs, water, salt and pepper. Pour egg mixture over all.
5. Bake in oven until frittata is golden brown and puffs up, about 30-45 minutes
6. Remove from oven, sprinkle with feta. Allow to sit for 10 minutes. Cut into wedges, serve and enjoy!

- Sue Stapp O'Donnell

Serves 8

Bull's Eye Egg

"My father began cooking these for the family as an interesting breakfast before we went out crabbing, or hiking, or sketching on the beach."

Sourdough bread

Eggs from island chickens

Butter

Homemade jam

1. With a cookie cutter, press a hole in the middle of the bread.
2. Heat a skillet over medium-low and melt butter. Place bread in skillet and crack the egg into the center of the bread.
3. Cook until the egg sets a bit on the bottom. After about 1 minute, flip over and cook until desired doneness. Serve with jam as desired.

- Carol Steffy

Serves 1

Guemes Island Crab Omelet

"I created this breakfast recipe for our out-of-town guests who swore that the only way to eat fresh crab was to dip it in Thousand Island dressing! My crab omelet not only dispelled that idea, but was also premiered on the KCTS Channel 9 "KCTS Cooks: Breakfasts." Make sure your crab is fresh and firm and follow it up with a blueberry parfait!"

1 cup chopped onions

1 cup sliced mushrooms

1 cup diced mixed-color bell pepper

2 tablespoons capers

Butter, as needed

2 cups cooked crab

1 cup shredded sharp cheddar cheese

1/2 cup shredded mozzarella cheese

6 eggs, beaten

1/4 cup half and half cream

1. In an oven proof skillet, preferably cast iron, sauté the onions, mushrooms, peppers and capers in butter, until soft, over medium heat.

2. Reduce heat to low. Add the crab and sauté quickly to coat with juices, but do not to over-cook it.

3. In a bowl, thoroughly mix eggs and cream. Pour the egg mixture over the crab sauté. Top with grated cheddar cheese, followed by mozzarella cheese. Turn on oven broiler.

4. Cook on low heat until the eggs begin to set up, but are not completely cooked.

5. Place the skillet in oven. Broil until the cheese is melted, bubbly, and slightly browned.

- Tim Wittman

Serves 4

Breakfast Avocado, Beans and Eggs

"Layers of avocado, beans and egg make this a healthy, hearty and delicious breakfast. "It's a mix of fresh avocado for fat, delicious pinto beans and other vegetables for slow-burning carbohydrates and topped with two farm fresh fried eggs for creamy deliciousness."

1 medium avocado, peeled and diced

1 tablespoon olive oil

1 tablespoon, garlic, minced

1 16-ounce can pinto beans, drained and rinsed

1 teaspoon red chili flakes

1/4 cup bacon crumbles, optional

1/4 cup chicken or vegetable broth

1 tablespoon vinegar

1 teaspoon avocado oil

2 eggs

2 tablespoons water

Salt and Pepper, to taste

1. Place avocado on plate and set aside. Crack two eggs in a dish and set aside.

2. In a medium frying pan, heat olive oil and garlic over medium high, about 1 minute, do not burn garlic. Add beans, chili flakes, bacon and stock cook until liquid is mostly evaporated.

3. With a wooden spoon, mash half the beans, leaving the other half whole, making for a blend of 'refried' and whole beans.

4. When most of the liquid is absorbed, make a clear space in bottom of frying pan. Add vinegar and reduce it a bit, then combine with bean mixture. Place beans on the bed of avocado.

5. In same pan, on medium-high, heat avocado oil. Add the eggs. When slightly set, add water and cover until eggs are done to your liking, about 1 minute.

6. Place eggs on top of beans, giving you a layer of avocado, beans and egg.

7. Salt and pepper, to taste.

- Eric Veal

Serves 1

Best Ever Granola

"Years ago a young hippie girl was living on Guemes and shared her granola recipe. I have changed the recipe through the years. Sometimes I add flax and chia seeds. The dried blueberries are a real treat. Melons are a nice addition."

6 cups regular rolled oats

2 cups large flaked coconut

1/2 cup raw sunflower seeds

1/2 cup pumpkin seeds

1/4 cup raw sesame seeds

1 cup each raw cashews, coarsely chopped

1 cup raw almonds, coarsely chopped

1 teaspoon cinnamon

2 tablespoons brown sugar, optional

1/2 cup vegetable oil

1/2 cup honey

3/4 cup raisins, craisins, or dried blueberries

1. Preheat oven to 325 degrees. Put first 8 ingredients in a 13"x9" pan and set aside.

2. In a small saucepan, over medium-low, heat oil and honey, but do not boil. Pour over dry ingredients and stir to coat.

3. Place in oven and cook for 1 hour, stirring occasionally. Granola should be nicely toasted.

4. Remove from oven to cool, stirring frequently to prevent sticking. Add raisins, craisins or dried blueberries. Serve with milk, yogurt, and fresh fruit. Store in an air-tight container.

- Janice Veal

12 cups

Anderson General Store Cinnamon Rolls

"Elaine couldn't make enough to satisfy the hungry weekend crowd. Shortly after Anderson's General Store opened in June of 1998, I started cooking there on weekends, using recipes from my cookbook, '6,000 Garlic Kisses.' It was immediately apparent that Elaine Anderson's Cinnamon Rolls were a huge hit. Soft, pillowy, the perfect amount of cinnamon, and that icing was to die for! And they were HUGE! Almost the size of dinner plates. Often people would split one four ways. You could only buy one per customer, unless you ordered the night before. Delish!" - Karen Everett

Cinnamon Rolls

2 cups buttermilk, warmed

1.5 ounces dry yeast, proofed

1 tablespoon sugar

1 1/2 cups butter, room temperature, divided

1 1/2 cup sugar, divided

1 teaspoon salt

1 egg

3 cups all purpose flour, divided

2 teaspoons cinnamon

Raisins and walnuts, as desired

Cream Cheese Frosting

8 ounces butter, room temperature

2 ounces cream cheese

1 1/2 cups of powdered sugar

1/2 cup heavy cream

1/2 tablespoons vanilla

1/2 teaspoon salt

1/4 teaspoon almond flavoring

1. In a medium bowl, combine 1/2 cup of warm buttermilk with 1 tablespoon of sugar. Stir in yeast and let sit until it foams.
2. In a standup mixer, combine 1 cup of butter and 1/2 cup of sugar, salt and remaining buttermilk.
3. Add yeast mixture and beat together at medium speed for 3 minutes.
4. Add egg and beat again until well mixed.
5. Add 2 cups of flour, beat at medium speed for another 3 minutes.
6. Put on the dough hook. Slowly add remaining 1 cup flour to make a soft dough. Knead for 5 minutes. Add more flour, as needed so not sticky. Turn out dough into a large greased bowl and turn once to grease top of dough ball.
7. Cover dough with a towel and let rise till double.
8. With a rolling pin, roll dough into a rectangle about 6" x 12" long, 1/2 to 3/4

inch thick. Paint rectangle with remaining 1/2 cup of softened butter.

9. Mix the remaining 1 cup of sugar with cinnamon and sprinkle over butter, then top with raisins and walnuts, as desired.

10. Roll up the rectangle, and slice into 6 sections about 1 inch wide and place into greased 9"x13" Pyrex pan. Let rise until doubled.

11. Bake at 350 degrees for about 40 minutes. Cool on wire rack.

Frosting

In a mixer, combine frosting ingredients, blend until smooth. Spread over cooled rolls. Frosting should partially melt over rolls.

- Elaine Anderson

Wild Rose Jelly

"I started making Wild Rose Jelly soon after coming to Guemes and seeing them everywhere. Wild Rose Jelly is a perfect complement to my Cooks Cove Scones (see page 144), pancakes, Dutch babies or crumpets.

1 quart rose petals

1 quart water

Juice of two lemons (this acts as pectin)

1 quart sugar

1. Select roses that you are sure are free of pesticides and are in the later stages of bloom. They are all over the island, if you don't have them in your yard, ask a neighbor if you can pick theirs.

2. Pull the petals off the stalks, and loosely fill a one-quart measuring jar. Cut off any white tips near the base. Rinse in cold water to make sure there are no bugs or dirt.

3. In a large pot, boil water, add rose petals, and simmer for 15 minutes. The lovely pink petals will turn into a mashing gray blob and you will question the process. Using a sieve, drain the water, catching the soggy petals in the sieve. Return liquid to the pot.

4. Now the magic happens. Add lemon juice, and the liquid turns to a vibrant pink color. Add one quart of sugar, and over medium heat, stir until dissolved. When the sugar has disappeared, bring to a boil until it reaches a setting point, 104°F.

5. Leave it to cool a little before bottling, foam will settle. Remove any remaining foam.

6. Pour jelly into jars that have been sterilized, filling 1/4 inch from the top of the jar. Wipe lip of jar before screwing on canning lids.

7. To can, submerge jars in water bath, boil for 10 minutes. This is unnecessary if you are going to use it right away.

- Mary Holmes

1 1/2 quarts

Cooks Cove Scones

"The smell of buttery scones, served with Wild Rose Jelly, strong coffee and a view of Cooks Cove is our family tradition. I have no idea what they taste like cold, as they never last long enough to find out."

3 cups all-purpose flour

1/2 cup granulated sugar

2 1/2 teaspoons baking powder

1/2 teaspoon baking soda

3/4 cup unsalted butter

1/2 teaspoon salt

2 tablespoons grated orange zest

3/4 cup dried fruit or berries (blueberries, apricots, cherries)

1/2 cup chopped nuts (pecans, almonds, walnuts)

1 cup buttermilk

Glaze

2 tablespoons heavy cream

2 teaspoons granulated sugar

1. Preheat oven to 425 degrees. In a large bowl, combine flour, salt and baking powder and baking soda. With a pastry blender or two knives, cut butter into dry ingredients, until butter is pebbly textured.

2. Add the orange zest, nuts and dried fruit of your choice and toss to combine. Stir in buttermilk until the dough is rough and shaggy.

3. Gather dough together and place on a generously floured work surface. Knead until ingredients are incorporated.

4. Divide dough in half and pat each piece into circle about 7 inches in diameter and 1/2 inch thick.

5. To glaze, brush each circle with the cream and sprinkle with sugar. Cut each round into eight pie-shaped wedges. Place the scones, barely touching, on baking sheet.

6. Bake until puffy and golden, 15 to 18 minutes.

- Mary Holmes

Makes 12

Cocoa Ripple Coffee Cake

"This yummy cake gets its name for the chocolate ripple running through it. Perfect with a cup of coffee or as a dessert."

1/2 cup butter, softened
3/4 cup sugar
2 eggs, beaten
2 teaspoons vanilla
1 1/2 cups sifted all-purpose flour
3/4 teaspoon salt
2 teaspoons baking powder
2/3 cup whole milk
1/2 cup Nesquik cocoa
1/3 cup chopped walnuts
Confectioners sugar, optional

1. Preheat oven to 350 degrees. Spray a 9"x9" pan or Bundt pan with non-stick oil.
2. In a medium bowl, cream together butter, sugar, eggs and vanilla until light and fluffy.
3. In another bowl, combine flour, salt and baking powder. Stir into butter mixture, alternate with milk, beating well after each addition.
4. Spoon 1/3 of batter into prepared pan, sprinkle with cocoa and walnuts. Repeat layers ending with batter.
5. Bake about 30 minutes, until a toothpick inserted into cake comes out clean. Let cake cool in pan for 10 minutes before inverting on a serving plate. Dust with confectioners sugar.

- Marge Kilbreath

Breads

Salmon BBQ at the Community Hall, 1955

Blueberry Boy Bait

"My husband, Don, loved to stop by Anderson's Blueberry Farm in Edison, and bring me recipes. This is a favorite. I have made it many times for Coffee Hour following the Church service."

2 cups flour

1 1/2 cup sugar

2/3 cup butter

2 teaspoons baking powder

1 teaspoon salt

2 eggs, separated

1 cup milk

1 cup blueberries

1. In a large bowl, sift flour and sugar together. Cut in the butter until size of small peas. Take out 3/4 cup for topping and set aside.

2. To the large bowl, add baking powder, salt, egg yolks, and milk and beat on low speed for 3 minutes.

3. In a small bowl, beat egg whites until stiff. Fold into batter and spread into a well-greased 12"x8"x2" or 13"x9"x2" inch pan. Evenly distribute blueberries over batter and sprinkle with reserved crumb topping.

4. Bake at 350 degrees for 40 to 50 minutes. Serve with whipped cream or plain as coffee cake.

- Julie Pingree

Serves 12

Swedish Braided Cardamon Bread

"This sweet bread is good with a meal and by itself. I sometimes eat it as dessert with butter. To make it your own, add spices of your choice, such as cinnamon, nutmeg or cloves."

2 cups whole milk

2/3 cup granulated sugar

1/2 cup butter

2 packets active dry yeast

6 cups all-purpose flour, divided

1 teaspoon salt

3/4 teaspoon ground cardamon

2 large eggs, divided

1 tablespoon whole milk

2 tablespoons Swedish pearl sugar, optional

1. In a small saucepan, combine milk and sugar until sugar dissolves. Add butter and stir over medium heat until butter is melted. Remove from heat and cool to lukewarm.

2. Stir in yeast and allow mixture to sit for 5 minutes, until bubbles appear on surface.

3. In a standup mixing bowl, fitted with dough hook attachment, pour in milk mixture. Add 2 cups of flour, salt, cardamon and 1 egg. Mix until combined.

4. Slowly add 3 more cups of flour and mix until completely combined. Add the remaining 1 cup of flour, a little at a time, until the dough forms a ball and no longer sticky. You might not use the entire cup.

5. Place the dough in a large, lightly oiled bowl. Cover with plastic wrap and let it rise in a warm spot until doubled in size, about an hour.

6. Punch down the dough. On a well floured surface, knead for about 2 minutes. Let rest for 10 minutes.

7. Divide dough into six equal portions. Roll each portion into a skinny rope, about 15 inches long. Line up 3 dough ropes, side by side. Pinch one end of the 3 ropes together, then gently braid together into a loaf. When at the end, pinch the three strands together and tuck ends under the loaf. Then tuck the first ends under the top of loaf. Repeat with remaining ropes to make a second loaf.

8. Place each loaf on a parchment lined baking sheet and let rise for 30 minutes. Preheat oven to 375 degrees.

9. To make egg wash, in a small bowl, whisk together remaining 1 egg and milk. If desired, sprinkle each loaf with the pearl sugar.

10. Bake loaves until browned on top, about 20 minutes. Remove to a wire pan, cool before slicing.

- Carol Deach

2 loaves

Beer Bread

"This recipe was one my mother shared with me many years ago and we always have it on St. Patrick's Day. I started volunteering with 'Guemes Connects' about 14 years ago; cooking alongside many other wonderful island cooks who make it possible to offer 'The Gathering Lunch' and 'Soup-To-Go.' This bread has been served many times to our Guemes Islanders."

3 cups self-rising flour

3 tablespoon sugar

1 12-ounce can of Guinness beer**

1. Preheat oven to 350 degrees. Place can of beer in a pan of warm water (beer needs to be warmer than room temperature). ** You can use any kind of beer, but I prefer Guinness which gives the bread a hearty flavor.
2. Spray bread pan (8"x4") with Pam. In a large bowl, combine flour and sugar. With a spoon, mix in warmed beer. Do not use beaters.
3. Pour dough into bread pan. Bake for 1 hour. Remove bread from pan and cool on a rack. Great sliced for toast.

- Lorraine Francis

1 loaf

Praline Muffins

"This originally came out of New Orleans from a friend that spent time down there working for FEMA after one of the big hurricanes about 10 years ago. Easy to make and really tasty."

2 cups brown sugar

1 cup flour

1 1/3 cups melted butter

4 eggs, beaten

2 cups chopped toasted pecans

1. Preheat oven to 350 degrees. Line miniature muffin tins with cupcake liners.
2. In a small bowl, mix the first 4 ingredients together. Stir in the pecans.
3. Spoon batter into tins. Bake for 20 minutes. (If using large muffin tin, bake for 28 minutes.)

- David McKibben

24 small muffins

Lemon Bread

"Serve this bread with raspberries, or any kind of berry, and a good cup of coffee or tea. Can't be beat. If you want to freeze bread, frost after thawing."

3 large eggs

1 1/4 cup sugar

1 cup sour cream

1/2 cup canola oil

2 tablespoons lemon zest

3 tablespoons lemon juice

1 1/2 cup flour

2 teaspoons baking powder

1/2 teaspoon salt

Frostings, see below

1. Preheat oven to 350 degrees. In a mixing bowl, combine eggs, sugar, sour cream, and oil. When smooth, add lemon zest and lemon juice and blend well.

2. In a small bowl, combine flour, baking powder and salt. Add to egg mixture. Stir until just combined. Do not over mix, may have some lumps.

3. Pour into parchment lined prepared loaf pans. Bake for 30 to 35 minutes. Cool in pan 10 minutes before turning out on a wire rack.

4. Use two frostings on this bread:

   Thin frosting, goes on warm loaves: Combine 1 cup powdered sugar, 2 tablespoons lemon juice. Add additional juice, as needed.

   Thick frosting, goes on cooled bread: Combine 1 cup powdered sugar, 1 tablespoon lemon juice. Add additional juice, as needed. Frosting can go on smoothly or even drizzle down the sides.

- Judy Rainwater

3 loaves (3"x5"pans) or 1 loaf (regular sized pan)

Zucchini or Pumpkin Bread

"Bob and I have been on Guemes since 1967. You may know Bob from Holiday Bazaars selling his beautiful wood carvings. Enjoy this versatile quick bread."

2 teaspoons baking powder

2 teaspoons baking soda

1 teaspoon salt

1/2 teaspoon nutmeg

1/4 teaspoon granulated ginger

1/4 teaspoon cardamon

1/4 teaspoon cloves

1 1/2 teaspoons cinnamon

1 cup chopped walnuts

1 cup Craisins

3/4 cup canola or vegetable oil

1 1/4 cups granulated sugar

1 1/4 cups brown sugar

3 eggs, beaten

2 1/4 cups zucchini or 15-ounce can pumpkin

2/3 cup buttermilk (or add 1 tablespoon vinegar to 2/3 cup regular milk and let sit a few minutes to sour)

3 1/2 cups flour (can use 1/2 cup whole wheat flour as part)

Raw sugar

1. Preheat oven to 350 degrees. In a large bowl, combine all dry ingredients. Add walnuts and Craisins.

2. In a mixer, beat together oil and sugars.

3. To the sugar mixture, add eggs beating well. Add the zucchini (or pumpkin) and mix well.

4. Add buttermilk and flour alternately to the mixing bowl, mix well.

5. Pour into parchment lined loaf pans. Sprinkle with a light amount of raw sugar.

6. Bake for 35 to 40 minutes, remove from oven. Cool on wire rack after removing from pan. Freezes well.

- Judy Rainwater

6 loaves (3"x5" pans) or 2 loaves (regular sized pans)

Dakota Bread

"Ready for a home spun treat? High on my list of comfort foods is a steaming bowl of clam chowder and a warm slice of freshly baked bread, slathered in butter. And none better to highlight island chowder than a slice of Dakota Bread. It is a light, nutty bread that merges varieties of wheat flour, oats, rye and sunflower oil, with a hint of sweetness. The recipe was created by the Dakota Wheat Commission."

1 package active dry yeast

1/2 cup warm water

2 tablespoons sunflower oil

1 egg

1/2 cup cottage cheese

1/4 cup honey

1 teaspoon salt

2 1/2 cups bread flour, more as needed

1/2 cup whole wheat flour

1/4 cup wheat germ

1/4 cup rye flour

1/4 cup rolled oats

Cornmeal

1 egg white, beaten

Topping

Wheat germ

Sunflower seeds

1. In a small bowl, mix the yeast in 1/2 cup warm water and dissolve. In a large bowl, mix the sunflower oil, egg, cottage cheese, honey, and salt. Add the dissolved yeast and mix again.

2. Add 2 cups bread flour and mix until it is well moistened. Gradually stir in the wheat flour, wheat germ, rye flour, and oats. Add enough bread flour to make the dough soft and pliable.

3. Turn out the dough on a floured surface and knead for about 10 minutes or until the dough is smooth. Place the dough in a greased bowl. Cover loosely with lightly oiled plastic wrap, let rise in a warm place until the dough doubles in size, about 45 minutes.

4. Punch down the dough, shape into one round loaf, place in a greased glass pie pan sprinkled with corn meal. Cover with lightly oiled plastic wrap and let rise until double in size, about 60 - 90 minutes. Preheat oven to 350 degrees.

5. Remove the plastic wrap and brush the dough with egg white. Sprinkle the top of the loaf with wheat germ and sunflower seeds. Bake for 35 to 40 minutes.

- Tim Wittman

1 loaf

Vegetable Jelly

"We came to the island as hippies during our 'back to the earth' phase and embraced island life. We respected island ways: we didn't insist community customs change nor expect the ferry schedule to change to suit our lifestyle. I was proud we could create a sweet spread with almost anything, including beets, berries, apples, peppers, pumpkins, and carrots. A favorite lunch consisted of homemade wheat bread with peanut butter spread to the edges and topped with whatever jelly we were featuring that day. My lovely, exotic mother-in-law, Olive Hoenselaar, sent me several unusual jelly recipes."

Beet Jelly

5 or 6 large beets, cleaned

Water

1/2 cup lemon juice

1 6-ounce package dry pectin

6 cups sugar

1. Place beets in a large pot and cover with water, bring to a boil, until tender. Remove and discard beets. Using cheese cloth, strain liquid and return to pot.
2. Add sugar to pot and enough water to make 4 cups of liquid. Bring to boil and then add lemon juice and pectin. Bring to boil again, add sugar and boil for 6 minutes. Pour into sterilized jars.

12 half pints

Green Pepper Jelly

3 large green bell peppers, cleaned and seeded

12 jalapeño peppers, cleaned and leaving a few seeds *(Be careful not to rub your eyes, you may want to wear surgical gloves.)*

1/2 cup water

3 cups vinegar

5 cups sugar

1 6-ounce bottle of Certo

Green food coloring, a couple drops

3. In a blender, finely grind peppers with water and vinegar.
4. In a large pot, combine pepper mixture with sugar and boil for 4 minutes. Add 6-ounce Certo and green food coloring, boil for another minute. Pour into sterilized jars.

- Barbara Hoenselaar
12 half pints

Caribbean Cornbread

"You will love this moist and sweet variation of cornbread. It works well as a side dish or with your morning coffee. Straight to you from the Caribbean."

2 teaspoons butter

2 teaspoons flour

1 cup all-purpose flour

1 cup coarse cornmeal

2 tablespoons baking powder

1 teaspoon salt

1/2 to 3/4 cup butter, room temperature

1/2 cup brown sugar

4 eggs

1 15.5-ounce can of corn, drained

1/2 to 2/3 cup of crushed pineapple, drained

1 cup shredded Monterey Jack or White Cheddar cheese

1. Preheat oven to 325 degrees.

2. Butter and flour a 9-inch square glass cake pan. In small bowl, whisk together flour, cornmeal, baking powder and salt; set aside.

3. In a medium bowl, using an electric mixer, cream butter and sugar together. While mixer is running, add eggs, one at a time, beating well after each addition.

4. Mix in corn, pineapple and cheese at low speed. Add flour mixture and mix until well blended.

5. Pour batter into prepared pan and bake until golden brown around edges and a tester inserted in the center comes out clean, about 1 hour or maybe less. Be sure to just check it!

- Leo E. Osborne

9 servings

Fresh Corn Coffee Cake

"I have many fond memories sharing this delicious, Costa Rican coffee cake with my study group. My friend's mother, 'Doña Fany,' would make it for us to enjoy during breaks from our study sessions."

3/4 cup flour

2 1/2 teaspoons of baking powder

8 ears of fresh corn (6 cups kernels)

1 14-ounce can sweetened condensed milk, divided

4 eggs, beaten

1/2 teaspoon vanilla extract

1/4 cup butter, melted

1/2 cup raisins, optional

1. Preheat oven to 350 degrees. Grease a 6-cup baking dish.

2. In a small bowl, sift together flour and baking powder.

3. In a food processor, blend corn and 1/2 cup milk. Pour through cheese cloth, separating liquid and solids. Discard solids. Pour strained liquid into a medium bowl.

4. To the strained liquid, stir in remaining condensed milk, eggs, vanilla, butter. Mix in flour and baking powder. Add raisins, if desired.

5. Pour mixture into prepared dish. Bake for 35 minutes or until a toothpick inserted in the middle comes out clean. Cut into desired sizes.

- Yadira Gonzales Young

Serves 6-8

Plum Bread

"Plum Bread is a Neilson family favorite for adults and kids alike. It is moist and sweet and works well as a breakfast bread, snack or dessert. It makes a great bundt cake, or a gift for family and friends during the holidays or any time."

2 cups flour

1 1/2 cup granulated sugar

1 teaspoon baking soda

1 teaspoon salt

1 teaspoon cinnamon

1/2 teaspoon nutmeg

1 cup salad oil

3 eggs, beaten

1 8-ounce jar Junior Baby Food Strained Plums

Topping

2 tablespoons margarine

1/4 cup granulated sugar

2 tablespoons milk

1/8 teaspoon baking soda

1. Preheat oven to 350 degrees. Grease 2 loaf pans or 1 Bundt pan.

2. In a medium bowl, mix together dry ingredients. Stir in oil and eggs.

3. With an electric beater on medium speed, mix in plums and beat for 2 minutes. Pour in pan(s).

4. Bake loaf pans for 35 to 40 minutes, Bundt pan for 45 to 50 minutes. Check if done by inserting a toothpick in the middle of bread and it comes out clean.

5. Remove from oven and allow to cool on wire rack. Wait about 10 minutes before inverting pans over a plate.

6. In a small saucepan over medium-low, bring topping ingredients to a boil for about 3 minutes, stirring constantly. Brush hot topping on warm cake.

- Dianne Neilson

2 loaf pans

1 Bundt pan

Blueberry Muffins

"I made these muffins for our weekend camping trips to Guemes. Everyone says these are the best blueberry muffins they've ever had."

1/2 cup rolled oats

1/2 cup orange juice

2 tablespoons sugar

1/4 teaspoon cinnamon

1 1/2 cups flour

1/2 cup sugar

1 1/4 teaspoon baking powder

1/4 teaspoon baking soda

1/2 teaspoon salt

1/2 cup cooking oil

1 egg, slightly beaten

1 cup blueberries

1. Preheat oven to 400 degrees. In a medium bowl, mix together oats and orange juice, set aside. In a small bowl, combine sugar and cinnamon, set aside.

2. In a large bowl, combine: flour, sugar, baking powder, baking soda, salt, oil and egg. Stir in oat and juice mixture. Gently fold in blueberries.

3. Fill muffin tins with mixture and top with cinnamon/sugar combination. Bake 18 to 20 minutes, until golden brown. Remove to a wire rack and allow to cool.

- Karon Monahan

12 muffins

Desserts

The last BBQ

Lemon Beach Pie

"In 1922 the area in Anacortes currently known as Washington Park or Sunset Beach, was destined for development. If not for a group of spirited Anacortes women, these 58 acres would likely be covered in homes. The women called themselves, 'The Anacortes Improvement Club,' and set about to purchase the property as a park and beach area for everyone to enjoy. The women contacted the City of Anacortes and proposed that if the city put up $1,500 they would put up the additional $1,000. A deal was struck. They began making Lemon Pies and the first day sales earned a whopping $300. The rest is history, as they say, and the goal was finally reached. The lemon filling recipe below was from Edna Truax of Anacortes."

1 tablespoon flour

3/4 cup water

Juice and zest of 1 lemon

1 1/4 cup sugar, divided

3 eggs, separated

1 pie crust, pre-baked

Mix flour and water, then combine with egg yolks, 1 cup of sugar, lemon juice and lemon rind. Cook in a double boiler until thick. Pour into pie crust. Beat the egg whites, adding remaing 1/4 cup of sugar, until stiff. Spread over lemon filling and brown in the oven.

- Anacortes Historical Museum

- Tim Wittman

Serves 8

Pie Crust

"Jane Read gave me this recipe in 2007."

4 cups unsifted flour

1 3/4 cup shortening

1 teaspoon sugar

2 teaspoon salt

1 tablespoon vinegar

1 egg

1/2 cup water

In a medium bowl, combine liquids to dry ingredients. Cover and chill before using.

- Bea Cashetta

5 single crusts

Meringue Pie

"Out of all my cooking over the years this 'air pie' continues to get rave reviews and recipe requests. It's cool, light and the perfect end to any meal. When you spread the whipped cream over the meringue, it won't look like enough. Magic is performed while it is refrigerated."

4 egg whites

1 cup sugar

1/4 teaspoon cream of tartar

1 cup whipping cream

1/2 teaspoon vanilla

2 squares unsweetened chocolate, grated

1. Preheat oven to 275 degrees. In a standup mixer, beat egg whites until they hold shape. Mix in tartar and gradually add the sugar until mixture is stiff and glossy.

2. Spread into a greased and floured 9-inch pie pan and bake for 20 minutes.

3. Turn the heat up to 300 to 325 degrees and bake for another 40 minutes. Remove from oven to cool. It will fall and that's normal.

4. In a standup mixer, whip the cream until stiff, then beat in vanilla. Spread the mixture over the entire top of the meringue. Sprinkle the chocolate over the cream mixture.

5. Refrigerate 10-24 hours. Enjoy!

- Patsi Waller

Serves 8

Fail Safe Pie Crust

"My in-laws, Bonnie and Cy Flory, built their Holiday Hideaway dream home in the mid 1990's. Bonnie's pies were legendary and thankfully she shared this recipe with me. This pastry is good for pies, tartlets and appetizers. If baking as a shell, the pastry has a tendency to puff up; so prick, generously, with a fork and bake with another pie tin on top of pastry for about 10 to 12 minutes."

5 cups flour

1 tablespoon brown sugar

1 teaspoon salt

1/2 teaspoon baking powder

2 cups shortening

1 egg, beaten

Water, as needed

1 tablespoon vinegar

1. In a medium bowl, combine first four ingredients. Cut shortening into flour mixture, until pea sized pieces.

2. In another bowl, combine egg, and enough water to make 3/4 cup liquid. Add vinegar.

3. Combine wet and dry ingredients. Work into a big ball.

4. Divide big ball into 6 to 8-inch fist sized balls. Roll out each ball, using a covered rolling pin on a pastry cloth. Mixture will take a lot of handling and still be flaky. Dough keeps 3 weeks refrigerated, 3 months frozen.

5. To bake, pre-heat oven to 450 degrees. Bake pie shell for 10 minutes at 450 degrees, then reduce to 350 degrees and bake for 20 to 40 minutes more or until filling is bubbly.

For an apple pie, use 4 to 6 Granny Smith apples, peeled, cored, sliced, toss with 2/3 cup white granulated sugar, with about 1 tablespoon cinnamon sprinkled, to taste.

- Deb Flory

3 to 4 double-crust pies

Wild Blackberry and Rhubarb Pie

"Islanders know (and rarely share) the sacred locations to harvest the tiny, tart, black jewels. In my opinion, too perfect to cook or bake! For anyone lucky enough to score some, just sprinkle over ice cream. But, recently, Bud shared this pie and it has become a favorite." - Tara Dowd.

1 box Pillsbury pie crusts

3/4 to 7/8 cup sugar, depending on how sweet the berries

2 to 3 tablespoons corn starch

4 cups of wild blackberries

2 cups sliced (1/4 inch pieces) rhubarb

2 tablespoons butter, divided

1 tablespoon granulated sugar

1 egg, beaten

Ice cream or whipped cream

1. Preheat oven to 425 degrees. Carefully place one crust into a nine-inch pie dish, overlapping the edge, stretching as necessary; set aside. Place cleaned berries and rhubarb in a large bowl.

2. In a medium bowl, combine sugar and cornstarch, pour dry mixture over fruit and gently mix to coat. Pour filling into the pie crust and dot with butter.

3. Place top crust over filling, fold top crust over the bottom crust and crimp edges, to prevent the juices from flowing over.

4. Score top crust to vent during baking. Brush top with beaten egg and sprinkle with sugar. Bake at 425 degrees for 35 minutes.

5. Reduce heat to 400 degrees and bake for 18 minutes more. Let rest for at least an hour. When serving, top with vanilla ice cream or whipping cream, if desired.

- Bud Ashbach

Serves 8

Cranberry Cornmeal Cake

"Vicki and Chuck served this Italian dessert at a recent dinner party. It is quick, easy and so yummy."

1 1/2 cups dried cranberries

3/4 cup cake flour, plus extra for dusting pan

3/4 cup fine yellow cornmeal

1 teaspoon baking powder

3 tablespoons orange zest (2 large oranges)

3/4 cup (1 1/2 sticks) salted butter, at room temperature, plus extra for buttering pan

1 1/4 cups sugar

1/2 teaspoon pure vanilla extract

4 large egg yolks

2 large eggs

1/3 cup fresh orange juice

Powdered sugar

1. Place rack in center of the oven. Preheat the oven to 350 degrees. Butter and flour an 8" round cake pan.

2. Place the cranberries in a sieve set over a medium bowl. Spoon flour over the cranberries and sieve the flour into bowl. Set flour-dusted cranberries aside.

3. To the flour, stir in cornmeal, baking powder and orange zest.

4. In a separate bowl, beat in butter and sugar until light and fluffy, about 3 minutes. Mix in vanilla. Continue mixing and one at a time, add egg yolks and whole eggs. Reduce the speed to low and add orange juice. Add flour mixture and combine until just incorporated. Fold in cranberries.

5. Pour batter into prepared cake pan and smooth the surface with a spatula. Bake until cake is golden and center is set, about 45 minutes. Transfer pan to a wire rack and let cool.

6. When cool, remove cake by tipping pan over onto rack. Dust with powdered sugar, if desired. Cut cake into wedges and serve.

- Vicki and Chuck Hallingstad

Serves 8

Zucchini Spice Cake

"This flavorful cake recipe was first published in the October 2014, Guemes Tide. *Use unpeeled, seeded zucchini. A great way to use those large zucchini that hide in your garden. Can be served with cooked apples, peach slices or a dollop of ice cream. It freezes well."*

1 cup canola oil

2 cups sugar

3 eggs

2 cups grated zucchini

3 teaspoons vanilla

3 cups flour

4 teaspoons cinnamon

1 teaspoon baking soda

1/2 teaspoon baking powder

1/2 cup chopped nuts, optional

1. Grease and flour a bundt or angel food cake pan. Preheat oven to 350 degrees.

2. In a large bowl, beat oil and sugar together. Add eggs and beat until light and fluffy. Add zucchini and vanilla and mix gently.

3. In a separate bowl, mix together dry ingredients, then add to zucchini mixture and mix thoroughly. Add nuts, if desired. Pour into prepared pan and bake for 1 hour.

4. Cool on a wire rack for 15 to 20 minutes, then remove cake from pan to cool.

- Lorraine Francis

12-15 servings

Chocolate Zucchini Cake

"Lorraine is famous for her baking. This cake is popular at 'Gathering Lunches' and bake sales."

2 1/2 cups flour

1/2 cup cocoa

2 1/2 teaspoons baking powder

1 1/2 teaspoons baking soda

1 teaspoon salt

1 teaspoon cinnamon

3/4 cup soft butter

2 cups sugar

3 eggs

2 teaspoons vanilla

3 teaspoons grated orange zest

2 cups shredded zucchini, unpeeled and seeded

1/2 cup milk

1 cup chopped pecans or walnuts, optional

Glaze
2 cups powdered sugar

3 tablespoons milk.

In a small bowl, mix sugar and milk until blended and smooth.

1. Preheat oven to 350 degrees. In a medium bowl, combine flour, cocoa, baking powder, baking soda, salt and cinnamon; set aside.

2. In a large bowl, use an electric mixer to beat together the butter and sugar until well blended. Add eggs one at a time, beating after each addition.

3. With a spoon stir in the vanilla, orange peel and zucchini. Alternately stir the dry ingredients and the milk into the zucchini mixture. Add nuts, if desired.

4. Pour the batter into a greased and flour dusted 10" tube pan or Bundt pan. Bake at 350 for an hour or until a wooden toothpick inserted comes out clean. Prepare glaze, if desired, by mixing all ingredients until blended and smooth.

5. Cool in the pan for at least 15 minutes, then turn it out onto a wire rack to cool. Drizzle with glaze or serve with vanilla ice cream.

- Lorraine Francis

Serves 12

Moist Chocolate Layered Cake

"No birthday is complete without this Fox family favorite. I took a standard recipe and made enough changes to call it my own. Several family members have dietary restrictions and appreciate the lack of gluten and dairy. This is a dense, full of chocolate flavor, not overly sweet, delicious cake - gluten and dairy-free. Ask any Fox!"

Cake

2 cups almond flour

3/4 cup white sugar

1/4 cup brown sugar

1/2 teaspoon salt

2 teaspoon baking powder

1 teaspoon xanthan gum powder

8 eggs, beaten

1/2 cup coconut or almond milk

2/3 cup Volupta Organic cocoa powder

1 cup coconut oil, melted and slightly cooled

2 teaspoon vanilla

3/4 cup semi-sweet chocolate chips, optional

Frosting

1 can of cold coconut cream (not coconut milk!)

1 teaspoon vanilla

1/2 cup berries, optional

1. Preheat oven to 350 degrees. In a medium bowl, whisk together dry ingredients.
2. In a separate large bowl, combine eggs, milk, cocoa powder, coconut oil and vanilla. With a mixer on medium, beat until blended.
3. Add dry ingredients and beat until smooth. Stir in chocolate chips, if desired.
4. Use cake pans with removable bottoms, cut parchment paper to size to cover bottoms. Spray avocado oil on sides and parchment paper. And just in case, place a sheet pan underneath the cake pans.
5. Transfer batter to prepared cake pans, trying to be sure same amount is in each one. Bake for 30 minutes. Remove from oven and cool on wire rack.
6. To make frosting: In a small bowl, whip together coconut cream and vanilla. Spread on frosting to create layered cake. Top with berries, if desired.

- Susie Fox

Serves 10

Raw Apple Cake

"My mother, Florence Nugent, made this family favorite cake. Having lots of apple trees, this has become a fall tradition to take to island potlucks. You may make it days early as the flavor improves. It may be topped with powdered sugar, ice cream, chocolate or vanilla frosting, or warm lemon sauce."

4 cups cubed apples, cored (peeled optional)

2 eggs

1/2 cup oil

1 1/2 teaspoons baking soda

1 teaspoon salt

1 1/2 teaspoons vanilla

1 1/2 teaspoons cinnamon

2/3 cup chopped walnuts

2 cups granulated or brown sugar

1 1/2 cups chopped dates (optional)

2 cups flour (or gluten free flour)

1. Preheat oven to 375 degrees. In a large bowl, combine all ingredients, and mix well. Oil a 9"x13" pan.

2. Pour in cake batter and bake for 45 minutes.

3. Remove from oven, place on a wire rack to cool. Top as desired.

- Nancy Bush

Serves 10

Sopapilla Cheesecake

"For 15 years, this dessert has received rave reviews. It is great for potlucks. Recommend raw blue agave rather than sugar for the topping, as it adds a mild fruity taste. Make a day ahead."

1 teaspoon olive oil

1 8-ounce canister of Pillsbury Sheet Roll dough

2 8-ounce packages cream cheese, softened in microwave for 60 seconds

1 cup white sugar (cheese filling)

1 1/2 teaspoons vanilla extract

1 8-ounce canister of Pillsbury Crescent Roll dough

1/2 cup white sugar (topping)

1/2 cup melted butter

Honey or Raw Blue Agave for a fruitier flavor

1 teaspoon ground cinnamon

1. Preheat oven to 350 degrees. Using olive oil, prepare a 9"x 13"inch pan by covering sides and bottom. Unroll the Pillsbury Sheet roll dough and place in baking pan.

2. In medium bowl, combine the softened cream cheese with sugar and vanilla and beat until smooth. Evenly spread the cream cheese mixture over the dough in pan. Refrigerate 30 minutes to stiffen cream cheese.

3. Unroll the Pillsbury Crescent Roll dough and float it over the cream cheese, mixture.

4. In medium bowl, combine sugar and melted butter. Using a spatula, spread evenly over the top of the cream cheese layer.

5. Bake for 32 minutes or until the crescent dough has puffed and golden brown.

6. Remove cheesecake from oven and immediately drizzle honey and sprinkle the cinnamon. Spread with spatula if necessary.

7. Place in refrigerator to cool completely before cutting into squares. Overnight works best.

- Walt, Sandy and Samson (woof) Seifried

24 squares

New Jersey Cheesecake

"Bonita is a baker, 'extraordinaire,' at The Guemes Island General Store. She says this cheesecake can be frozen".

2 tablespoons oil

1 cup graham cracker crumbs

5 8-ounce packages cream cheese, room temperature

1 1/2 cups granulated sugar

3 tablespoons flour

1 1/2 teaspoons vanilla

1/2 teaspoon lemon zest

1/2 teaspoon orange zest

5 eggs

2 egg yolks

3/4 cup heavy cream

1/3 cup sour cream

1. With oil, generously grease sides and bottom of a 9-inch spring form pan. Dust with graham cracker crumbs. Pre-heat oven to 500 degrees.

2. In a medium bowl, cream together: cream cheese, sugar, flour, vanilla, lemon and orange zest. Add eggs and yolks, one at a time, blending after each addition.

3. Mix in heavy cream and sour cream.

4. Pour into prepared pan. Bake in a water bath at 500 degrees for 10 minutes. Reduce to 250 degrees and bake for 1 1/4 hour or until golden brown.

5. Remove from oven and cool on wire rack. Chill, covered, overnight.

- Bonita Smith

Serves 10

Chocolate Espresso Torte

"Walking into the Anacortes Yacht Club, I overheard the receptionist speaking to her mother in Italy. She shared this delicious recipe with me."

1 cup butter

1 cup plus 2 tablespoons sugar

1 cup plus 2 tablespoons espresso coffee

16 ounces semi-sweet chocolate (I use semi sweet chocolate chips)

6 eggs, room temperature

1 egg yolk, room temperature

1. Preheat oven to 325 degrees. Generously butter an 8" to 9" springform pan. Line the bottom with parchment paper, butter and flour, set aside.

2. In a heavy saucepan over medium low heat, melt butter, sugar together and add espresso. Cook together until sugar dissolves. Blend in chocolate and stir until smooth. Remove from heat.

3. In a bowl, whisk eggs and yolk until frothy. Blend eggs into warm chocolate mixture, a little at a time so not to cook the eggs. Pour batter into prepared spring form pan and place on a baking sheet and into the oven.

4. Bake about 1 hour, until edges puff and crack slightly, but center is not completely set, DO NOT OVERBAKE. Remove from oven, cake will continue to set as it cools.

5. Transfer pan to rack and allow cake to cool before removing from the pan. Cover and refrigerate overnight.

- David McKibben

Serves 10

Rustic Fruit Tart

"This is an easy, no fuss, open faced pie recipe. It can be used with different fruits as the seasons change. In Fall, use sliced apple with cranberries. In Winter use pear with pomegranate. In Spring, use rhubarb with raspberries. In Summer, berries. To make it even easier, roll out a pre-made pie crust."

Pastry

1 1/2 cups all-purpose flour

1/8 cup granulated sugar

1/2 teaspoon salt

2/3 cup butter cold unsalted butter, cut into 1/2 inch cubes

1 egg yolk

3 tablespoons cold milk

Filling

2 cups fresh raspberries

1 cup fresh blueberries

1 cup fresh blackberries

1/4 cup granulated sugar, maybe more, depending on the sweetness of the berries.

1 teaspoon lemon zest

1 tablespoon all-purpose flour

1/8 teaspoon salt

1 egg, beaten

1 tablespoon coarse sugar

1. To prepare pastry: In a standup mixer, combine flour, sugar and salt. Add the butter and mix on low until the the butter pieces are the size of peas, about 2 minutes.

2. In a small bowl, mix the egg yolk and milk. Add to the flour mixture and mix until the dough just comes together, about 30 seconds. It will look dry, but don't worry.

3. Turn onto clean counter, and knead about 2 minutes, use a scraper to pull it together. Roll into a flat disk, wrap in plastic wrap and refrigerate for 1 hour. Preheat oven to 350 degrees, place rack in middle of oven.

4. To prepare filling: In a large bowl, combine the raspberries, blueberries and blackberries, toss with sugar. Taste, if more tart than you like, add a bit more sugar. Stir in the lemon zest, flour and salt until evenly mixed.

5. To assemble: Remove dough from refrigerator and let rest for about 10 minutes. On a lightly floured board, roll the pastry into a 13 to 14-inch circle and transfer to a parchment lined, rimmed baking sheet.

6. Pile the fruit in the center, leaving a 2-inch border. Fold the corner up, over the filling, pleating and pressing gently. Brush the pastry with egg wash and sprinkle with sugar.

7. Bake about 40-55 minutes, or until crust is golden brown. Transfer the

baking sheet to a wire rack to cool. When cool, transfer to a serving plate.

- Lindsay Ashbach
Serves 8

Orange Almond Biscotti

"I have been making this recipe for decades. As a child, I learned it in my Chicago grandmother's kitchen. I always try adding new ingredients, but the orange almond is a favorite. This recipe is shared often, because it is so easy."

1 1/2 cups all-purpose flour, extra if needed

1 1/2 teaspoons baking powder

1/4 teaspoon salt

1 tablespoon orange zest

1 orange, juiced

1/2 cup coarsely chopped almonds

2 tablespoons unsalted butter

1/2 cup granulated sugar

1/4 cup honey, warmed

2 large eggs

1 teaspoon vanilla extract

1. Preheat oven to 325 degrees. Grease one large baking sheet.
2. In a medium bowl, combine flour, baking powder, salt, orange zest, orange juice and almonds. Set aside.
3. In a separate bowl, cream butter, sugar, honey, egg, and vanilla until smooth. Add dry ingredients and mix well.
4. Turn dough onto a well floured board. Divide dough into two equal pieces. Roll each piece of dough into a 12-inch log. Place logs 4 to 5-inches apart on prepared baking sheet. Flatten tops slightly.
5. Bake for 20 to 25 minutes or until firm. Remove from oven and when cool, cut logs diagonally into 1/2-inch slices.
6. Place slices on the baking sheet 1/2-inch apart and return to oven for 10 to 20 minutes or until lightly browned. Cool completely. Store in an airtight container.

- MJ Andrak
Approximately 24 pieces

Oatmeal Carmelita Bars

"We were looking for some yummy gluten-free cookies, Deanne came across these. She altered a couple of things, and they came out great! Gluten free!"

1 cup gluten-free all-purpose flour (We use Bob's Red Mill)

3/4 cup brown sugar

1/4 teaspoon sea salt

1 cup gluten-free oats

1/2 teaspoon baking soda

3/4 cup melted butter

1/4 teaspoon vanilla

1 1/2 cups gluten-free chocolate chips (We use 70% dark chocolate)

1/2 cup chopped pecans (can also use walnuts), optional

1 cup salted caramel sauce (cooled to room temperature *recipe below)

3 tablespoons gluten-free all-purpose flour

Salted Caramel Sauce

1 cup sugar

1/4 cup water

3/4 cup coconut cream

3 1/2 tablespoons unsalted butter

1 teaspoon salt

1. In a stand mixer, on low speed, mix the first seven ingredients together until it begins to form crumbs.

2. Press half of this mixture into the bottom of an 8"x8" inch square baking dish (reserve the other half for the topping).

3. Bake the crust at 350 degrees for 12 minutes. Remove from oven and sprinkle chocolate chips and chopped nuts over the crust as soon as it comes out of the oven.

4. To make caramel sauce: Combine sugar and water in a heavy saucepan over medium-low heat until sugar is completely dissolved. Slowly bring the sugar mixture to a boil and do not stir. Boil until the syrup becomes a rich amber color, about 5 to 6 minutes, making sure to scrape down the sides of the pot. Remove from the heat and quickly whisk in the heavy cream. Next, stir in the butter and salt. Transfer to a bowl to cool.

5. In a small bowl, combine the Salted Caramel Sauce and 3 tablespoons gluten-free flour with a whisk. Drizzle over nuts and chocolate chips. Sprinkle remaining crumbs over the top and bake for 15 to 20 minutes or until golden brown. Cool and serve.

- Beverly James and Deanne Savage

Serves 9

Mrs. Sigg's Snickerdoodles

"A favorite cookie at Guemes Island's 'Soup-to-Go' lunches."

1 1/2 cups sugar

1/2 cup room temperature butter

1/2 cup shortening

2 large eggs, room temperature

2 teaspoons vanilla

2-3/4 cups flour

2 teaspoons cream of tartar

1 teaspoon baking soda

1/4 teaspoon salt

2 tablespoons white sugar

2 teaspoons cinnamon

1. Preheat oven to 400 degrees. In a large bowl, blend until creamy: sugar through vanilla.

2. In a separate bowl combine dry ingredients (flour through salt). Slowly, beat in creamed ingredients. Grease two baking sheets.

3. Shape dough into balls about the size of a walnut. In a small bowl, combine sugar and cinnamon.

4. Roll balls in cinnamon and sugar mixture. (A baggie works great.) Place balls on baking sheets.

5. Bake 8-10 minutes, switching racks halfway through.

6. Remove from the oven and transfer to wire racks to cool and Enjoy!

- Toni Schmokel and Sharon Huglitt

3 to 4 dozen cookies

Lemon Glazed Lemon Crisps

"These cookies are served with 'Soup-to-Go,' favorites, Irish Potato Leek Soup and Beer Bread."

Cookie
1-1/2 cups sugar

1 cup softened butter

2 eggs

3 tablespoons sour cream

1 teaspoon vanilla

3-1/4 cups flour

1/2 teaspoon baking soda

1/2 teaspoon salt

Powdered sugar

Lemon Glaze
2 cups powdered sugar

3 tablespoons lemon juice

2 teaspoons lemon zest

1. In large bowl, beat sugar and butter until fluffy. Beat in eggs, sour cream and vanilla. Combine flour, soda and salt; stir into sugar mixture. Cover and chill for 30 minutes or more.

2. Preheat oven to 375 degrees. On a powdered sugar covered board, roll out half of dough to 1/8 inch thick. Using cookies cutters, cut out various shapes. Place 1 inch apart on cookie sheet. Bake 10 to 12 minutes. Cool on rack.

3. Lemon Glaze: In a small saucepan, over low heat, combine lemon juice and powdered sugar. Mix in lemon zest, cool slightly. Drizzle glaze over cookies.

- Lorraine Francis

6 dozen

Pineapple Cookies

"My mother taught our Bluebird troop how to make these cookies in 1961. They have been a family favorite ever since."

1 cup shortening or softened butter

1 cup brown sugar

1 cup granulated sugar

2 large eggs

1 1/2 teaspoons vanilla

1 8 3/4-ounce can crushed pineapple, drained (reserve juice)

4 cups all-purpose flour

1 teaspoon baking soda

2 teaspoons cream of tartar

1/2 teaspoon salt

1/4 teaspoon nutmeg

1/4 cup slivered almonds

1. Preheat oven to 375 degrees. In a medium bowl, cream together first 6 ingredients.

2. In a larger bowl, sift together flour, baking soda, cream of tartar, salt and nutmeg.

3. Slowly, stir in wet ingredients until well blended. Mix in the nuts. If dough feels too dry and crumbly, add one ot two tablespoosn of the reserved pineapple juice.

4. Scoop a heaping tablespoon of dough on parchment lined cookie sheets, 2 inches apart.

5. Bake 8 to 10 minutes until edges begin to turn brown. Remove from oven and cool on a wire rack. The cookie has an almost cake-like texture.

- Pat Richley-Erickson

2 to 3 dozen cookies

Chocolate Macaroons

"This cookie recipe was originally available in San Juan Classics II. *Such a favorite, I wanted to include in the GIHS cookbook."* - Dawn Ashbach

3 ounces unsweetened chocolate

4 egg whites, room temperature

1/2 teaspoon salt

1 1/2 cup granulated sugar

2 tablespoons white flour

1 teaspoon vanilla extract

3 cups shredded coconut

1. Preheat oven to 325 degrees. In a small bowl melt chocolate in microwave and set aside. In a small bowl, combine, salt, sugar and flour.
2. In a stand up mixer, beat egg whites until foamy. (Don't over beat or egg whites will separate.) Gradually add sugar mixture, continually beating, until mixture holds stiff peaks.
3. Stir in vanilla and warm, melted chocolate. Gently, fold in coconut.
4. Line large baking sheets with parchment paper. Using a teaspoon, drop batter onto paper, 2-inches apart. Bake for 20 minutes.
5. Remove from oven and allow to rest for 5 minutes. Using a spatula, transfer cookies to a wire rack. When cool, store in a covered container.

- San Juan Classics Cookbook II

2 dozen cookies

Bill's Flan, from his Misspent Youth

"Bill and Stephanie brought this to a Guemes Historical Society Meeting. So good, highly recommend."

6 eggs

6 tablespoons sugar

2 cups heavy cream

1 teaspoon vanilla

1/3 cup white sugar

1. Preheat oven to 350 degrees. In a medium bowl, thoroughly combine eggs and sugar. Mix in cream and vanilla. Set custard mixture aside.

2. Water bath: Place an empty 9" pie pan in a larger pan. To approximate the water amount needed in the 'water bath,' in large pan, pour water around pie pan. Remove pie pan. Pour the water into the pot and bring to a boil, add a cup or so for good measure. The water bath needs to be as hot as possible.

3. Place pie pan in the oven to warm.

4. Place 1/3 cup of sugar in a small frying pan and heat under moderate heat. Sugar will melt and become caramel. Shake pan, don't stir.

5. When the caramel is ready, take the pie pan out of the oven and pour in the hot caramel.

6. Pour the custard mixture over the caramel.

7. Place the empty, large pan in oven. Carefully place the filled pie pan into the large pan.

8. Add boiling water to the large pan up to around 1/2 inch or so to the top of pie pan.

9. Bake for about 25 minutes and then check if done by gently shaking; the center should jiggle slightly. Remove from oven, cover and let sit for an hour, then refrigerate until cold.

10. To serve: Remove from refrigerator and remove cover. Run a knife around the edges to separate the custard from the dish. Place a large plate, serving side down, over pie pan and quickly turn upside down. Slice to serve. Lick the knife. Yum.

- Bill Van Vlack

Serves 8

Raspberry Ribbon Dessert

"This recipe is from my mom, Alice Shoultz. It is a favorite at family gatherings."

Crust
8 tablespoons butter, room temperature

1/4 cup sugar

2 cups graham cracker crumbs

Jello Mixture
1 package 6-ounce package raspberry jello

2 teaspoon lemon juice

2 cups water, boiling

2 1/2 cups packages frozen raspberries

Whipped Cream Topping
2 3-ounce packages cream cheese, room temperature

1/2 cup sugar

1 teaspoon vanilla

2 cups whipped cream

1. To make graham cracker crust: in a medium bowl, combine butter, sugar and graham cracker crumbs. Place in bottom of a 9x12 inch pan. Reserve some to sprinkle on top.

2. To make jello mixture: in a medium bowl, combine raspberry jello, lemon juice and boiling water. Stir in frozen raspberries and place bowl in refrigerator to cool and thicken. Stir occasionally to ensure raspberries are mixed throughout.

3. When jello mixture is thickened, not set, pour over graham cracker crust. Return to refrigerator.

4. Whipped cream topping: In a medium bowl, beat cream cheese, sugar and vanilla together. Fold in whipped cream.

5. When jello is set, spread topping. Sprinkle with some of the graham cracker mixture.

- Carol Deach

Serves 10

Lemon Fluff

"We are happy to share this yummy, easy pie. It has been served at many a Guemes gathering. The whipped jello mixture can be used as a fruit topping. It was previously printed in the Guemes Tide 2013.*"*

1 small box lemon jello

1 3/4 cup hot water

3/4 cup sugar

Juice and zest of one lemon

1 can evaporated milk, chilled

Graham cracker crust

1. In a medium bowl, combine first four ingredients. Chill until thickly jelled, but not set.

2. In a separate bowl, whip evaporated milk until soft peaks form.

3. Fold jello mixture into whipped milk. Continue to whip until blended and thick.

4. Spoon over graham cracker crust. Refrigerate for at least an hour.

- Dave Rockwood and Wendy Savers

Serves 8

Divine Nut Butter with Coconut and Cardamom

"I bought this nut butter in Portland, Oregon and it blew my mind. I have recreated it and always have it on hand for putting on my bread, apple slices and pancakes."

10 1/2 ounces almonds

6 ounces cashews

1/3 cup unsweetened coconut flakes

1 teaspoon flax seed

1 1/2 tablespoon chia seeds (not ground)

2 teaspoon ground cardamom

3/4 teaspoon salt

2 tablespoons honey

1 to 3 tablespoons avocado oil, as desired

1. In a food processor, blend almonds, cashews and coconut until the consistency of peanut butter, about 10 minutes. Scrape down sides of blender, occasionally. The butter should be completely smooth, not gritty or tacky.

2. Add remaining ingredients and mix until just combined. If not as smooth as desired, stir in oil by hand.

3. Store in a covered jar, unrefrigerated. Enjoy!

Tips

Don't give up. There will be a couple of minutes where the recipe will look like it's not going to work. Within the first few minutes, the nuts will be ground into a fine powder, and eventually create a crumbly ball. It may seem as though your nut butter may never fully "butter." But keep machine running because within just a few more minutes, the dry mixture will release enough oils that a creamy spread will begin to form and swirl. It's like magic.

Don't: Add any liquids, it will cause the butter to clump.

Do: Add oil, if desired. If butter is too thick for your liking, by hand, blend in a little bit of oil. Leave this as very last step as it's often unnecessary.

- Diana Lind

2 1/2 cups

Raspberry Cordial

"Enjoy a taste of summer on a cold winter night, in front of the fireplace. My mother-in-law, Claudia Ashbach shared this recipe."

3 quarts raspberries, fresh or frozen

2 cups granulated sugar

1 quart vodka

1. Place raspberries in a gallon jar and crush using a potato masher. Mix in the sugar and vodka.

2. Let stand, unrefrigerated, for 8 weeks. Stir everyday for the first week and once a week thereafter.

3. Using a couple layers of cheese cloth and a colander, strain the juice from the pulp, into a large pot. (Claudia used a nylon sock resting in a colander, which was placed in a large pot.) Do not squeeze the cheese cloth or sock. It is ready to bottle and be enjoyed.

4. If you have time and want to be sure you will have no sediment on the bottom of your bottles, you may add this step. After it is strained, pour the cordial into a gallon jar and let stand in a cool, dark place for 1 to 2 months. Using plastic surgical tubing, available at hardware stores, syphon the cordial into your bottles. Avoid letting the tube tip touch the sediment on the bottom. Enjoy!

- Claudia Ashbach

6 pints

Bourbon Slushie

"Best ever on a hot day. Enjoy!!"

7 cups water

5 plus cups of bourbon

12 ounces frozen lemonade

12 ounces frozen limeade

6 ounces orange juice

2 limes, juiced and zested

2 cups strong black tea

1. In a large freezer appropriate container(s), combine all ingredients.

2. Place in freezer. After 2-3 hours, stir so nothing settles.

3. Wait at least 24 hours, serve in individual glasses with a spoon.

- Melita Townsend

Serves a lot

Harvest Pie

"In 1999, I planted 175 quince trees, along with apples, pears, plums, cherries and aronia berries to start Willowrose Bay, a commercial, organic orchard on South Shore Road. It continues to supply stores and restaurants throughout western Washington."

Pastry for two-crust 9-inch pie

2 cups pears, peeled, cored and sliced

2 cups apples, peeled cored and sliced

2 cups quince, peeled cored and sliced (do last)

1 1/2 cups sugar, more to taste

1/8 teaspoon nutmeg

6 tablespoons flour

1/4 cup chopped crystalized ginger, optional

1 tablespoon butter

1. Preheat oven to 425 degrees.
2. Place fruits in a large bowl. In a medium bowl, mix together, sugar, nutmeg, flour and ginger (if desired) and combine with fruit.
3. Pour mixture into pastry lined pie plate, dot with butter. Cover with top pastry, seal and slice vent. Cover loosely with foil.
4. Bake for about 1 hour, until juice is bubbling and congealed. Remove foil and bake for about 10 more minutes, to brown crust.

- Edith Walden

8 servings

Pumpkin Cheesecake

"If you find a recipe you and everyone else loves, make it over and over again adding and changing flavors with the seasons. This is one such recipe. Enjoyed with friends over many years."

Crust
1 1/2 cups graham cracker crumbs

1/3 cup ground almonds

1/2 teaspoon ginger

1/2 teaspoon cinnamon

1/3 cup melted butter

Filling
4 8-ounce packages cream cheese, room temperature

1 1/4 cups granulated sugar

3 tablespoons maple syrup

3 tablespoons cognac

1 teaspoon cinnamon

1/4 teaspoon nutmeg

4 eggs, room temperature

1/4 cup whipping cream

1 cup cooked or canned pumpkin

Topping
2 cups sour cream

1/4 cup sugar

1 tablespoon maple syrup

1 tablespoon cognac

1/2 teaspoon ginger

1. Preheat oven to 425 degrees.

2. For crust: In a medium bowl, combine all ingredients and press in an even layer on bottom of a 10-inch springform pan. Bake for 10 minutes, remove from oven and place on a wire rack to cool. Reduce oven temperature to 325 degrees.

3. For filling: In a standup mixer, beat cream cheese until smooth. Gradually add sugar and beat until light and fluffy. Add maple syrup, cognac, ginger, cinnamon and nutmeg; blend well. Add eggs, 1 at a time, beating thoroughly after each addition. Add cream and pumpkin, mix well.

4. Pour filling onto prepared pie crust. Bake for 45 minutes. Turn oven off, do not open door for an hour. Remove from oven and let rest after 15 minutes.

5. Prepare topping: Preheat oven to 425 degrees. In a small bowl, blend together topping ingredients. Spread topping over cheesecake and bake for 10 minutes.

6. Allow to cool at room temperature for at least an hour, before serving.

- Barbara Hoenselaar

Desserts

Quince Jelly

"Quince fruit, while unfamiliar to many in the United States, is common in many cuisines around the world. Before commercial pectin, nearly every farm had a quince tree, because the fruit is high in pectin. When eaten raw, it has an acerbic taste, but when cooked, imagine the taste of an apple with the added flavors of pineapple and orange."

Quince

Sugar

Lemon juice

1. Wash quince and cut into pieces. Do not peel or core. Place in saucepan or pot and add water to just about cover. Bring to boil and then cover with lid. Simmer until the quince turns a rose color. Depending on the volume of quince, this may take up to several hours.

2. Strain liquid through a jelly bag, layers of cheese cloth or nylon mesh. Add an equal volume of sugar to the liquid.

3. Add 1 tablespoon of lemon juice per 3 cups of quince juice to the mixture.

4. In small batches, in a preserving pan or large open sauce pan, bring the mixture to a hard boil (skimming off foam as it forms). Continue until the liquid coats a metal spoon (soft ball stage on candy thermometer).

5. Pour into jars and seal.

- Edith Walden

First Prize Applesauce Cake

"My mom, Lil Cronkite, gave me this recipe on a 3"x5" recipe card that she 'typed,' so sweet. She would make this cake for holiday weekends, where the whole family would be at the cabin - tents and all. We would all enjoy a piece and then mom would cover the cake with foil and leave it on the kitchen counter...But as the evening wore on, the cake would get smaller and smaller (as people walked by and snuck another bite) and there was never much left in the morning."

1/2 tablespoon vegetable oil

1/2 tablespoon flour

4 cups flour

4 teaspoons soda

1 1/4 teaspoon salt

2 teaspoons cinnamon

1/2 teaspoon nutmeg

1/2 teaspoon cloves

2 tablespoons cocoa

1 cup vegetable oil

2 cups sugar

3 cups unsweetened applesauce, heated

1/2 cup raisins

1/2 cup chopped walnut

1. Preheat oven to 400 degrees. Oil and flour a 9"x13" pan.

2. Sift together next 7 ingredients into a large bowl. In a stand up mixer, combine oil and sugar and beat until well blended. Stir in applesauce, add dry ingredients and blend well. Fold in raisins and walnuts.

3. Turn batter into prepared baking pan. Bake at 400 degrees for 15 minutes, then reduce heat to 375 and bake 15 minutes longer or until a toothpick comes out clean.

4. Remove from oven and cool on a wire rack. Prepare frosting.

Caramel Frosting
1/2 cup butter

1 cup dark brown sugar, firmly packed

1/2 teaspoon salt

1/4 cup milk

2 cups white sugar

1. In a saucepan over low heat, melt butter. Stir in brown sugar and salt. Bring to a boil over medium heat. Boil 2 minutes, stirring constantly.

2. Remove from heat and stir in milk. Return to heat and bring to full boil. Remove from heat, cool to lukewarm and add 2 cups of sugar. Beat until smooth.

Quince Marmalade

"The first marmalade was made from quince. The word "marmalade" comes from the Portuguese word for quince, "marmelo.""

3 1/3 pounds quince

1 orange

4 1/2 pounds sugar

1 cup orange juice

2 cups water

1. Quarter and core quinces, do not peel. Quarter and seed orange, do not peel.

2. In a food processor, chop quinces and oranges into thin pieces. Place fruit in a large heavy bottomed cooking pot.

3. Add sugar, orange juice and water. Bring to a boil, stirring frequently. Simmer, stirring frequently until juice sheets from the spoon.

4. Pour into jars and seal.

- Edith Walden

About 11 cups

Anne McCracken's Crispy Oatmeal Cookies

"The McCrackens and the Everetts have been neighbors on North Beach for about 70 years. While Phil was a world-renowned sculptor and artist, Anne was pretty famous in her own right, as a schoolteacher and as a promoter of the Skagit River Poetry festival. She is also one of the sweetest ladies I've ever known, just like these cookies. They're very simple, only four ingredients."
 - Karen Everett

1 cup butter

1 cup sugar

1 cup flour

2 cups oatmeal (not quick cooking)

1. Preheat oven to 400 degrees.

2. In a mixing bowl, combine butter, sugar, flour and oatmeal. Anne told me to, "Work it around with your hands."

3. With a tablespoon make round balls, then flatten the ball a bit to form a pancake.

4. Place on ungreased cookie sheet and bake for 15 to 20 minutes.

- Karen Everett

2 dozen cookies

Appendix

"Planked" salmon barbecue, South Beach, 1951

1962 Cookbook

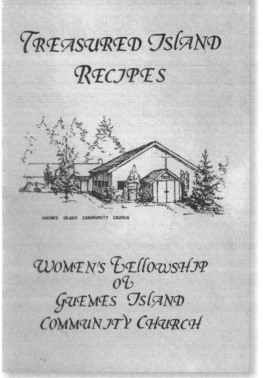

1972 Cookbook

Appendix

1962 and 1972 Cookbooks Cooks

1962

Thelma Benjestorf	Sigrid Trautman	Louise Pinneo
Isabelle Griggs	Gertie Howard	Ruth Tuttle
Rosemary Hammill	Helen Vonnegut	Alice Veal
Virginia Humble	Sarah Kingston	Mabel Fengler
Agnes Orsini	Maude Wooten	Hattie Kager
Ann Bessner		

1972

Claudia Ashbach	Rita Dewar	Anne McCracken
Laura Burton	Meta Whicker	Vivian Bush
Alice Shoultz	Betty Crookes	Gerry Dutton
Helen Trefethen	Dessie Weigel	Jane Veal Read
Linda Porter	Olive MacFetridge	Dot Graham
Judy Rainwater	Agnes Ashback	Mary Stapp

Favorite Recipes from Guemes Island Cooks

Compiled by the Women's Recreation Club of Guemes Island, 1962.

A bright August sun warmed the gathering of people on the south beach of Guemes Island. They moved in a line along a serving table made of silver-grey beach planks, taking portions of rosy salmon and homemade potato salad.

As they balanced themselves and their paper plates on driftwood perches, enjoying the panorama of Anacortes across the Channel, tasting the tender smoky salmon, they were participating in the making of a tradition. It was the first Guemes Island salmon barbecue, and the date was August 19, 1951.

A small Parent Teacher's Association group formed the committee, all of them young parents who had met that year, one evening each month, at the Guemes School, organizing an island P. T. A. unit with Walter Vonnegut, the teacher.

The parents had erected swings and teeter-totters on the school grounds, and hoped to provide a slide and a merry-go-round for the children's use. The barbecue was proposed as a means of raising funds for this equipment.

Bill Fast, one of the parents, offered to barbecue the salmon by the method the Lummi Indians had taught him while he and his wife were living on Lummi Island, operating a resort. And so it was done. The R. O. Clippingers gave permission for the use of their beach, just west of the ferry landing.

The women made salads, the men gathered drift wood for the fires and planks for the fish. And assisted Bill with the night-before filleting and salting of the salmon. On the morning of the barbecue, the racks of planked salmon attracted the gathering crowd long before they were pronounced ready by Bill in his tall chef's cap.

It certainly "tasted like more" and there was more, each year, with crowds and enthusiasm growing steadily. The playground was furnished and a cooperative island kindergarten was supported, as well, by the barbecue funds.

By 1953, the original committee realized it had a tiger by the tail, and asked the Community Club for assistance. For a time the event was a joint project of the two groups, who shared both the preparations and the proceeds. After 1954, the P.T. A group, having reached its goals (summer visitors to the island often bring their children to the school playground with its slide, merry-go-round and swings) withdrew entirely. The Community Club now sponsors the barbecue, held each year on the Sunday before Labor Day.

In 1954, a pouring rain forced a crisis decision: the barbecue was moved indoors to the Community Hall, and the salmon racks set up just south of the building. The impromptu arrangements were so satisfactory that the barbecue never went back to the beach. Bill Fast continued as chef until he moved away, when the committee asked Walter Vonnegut to take over. So popular is the event that no matter how many pounds of salmon are prepared, there never is enough.

The barbecue is now the Event of the Year to the hardworking committees - Country Store, Pie Booth, Decorations, Buying, Serving, Coffeemaking, Clean-Up - and also to the appreciative visitors who enjoy the charming island setting and the atmosphere of the barbecue done in its very special way.

BAR-B-Q Salmon Recipe

Filet salmon and nail the sides on a slab of beach drift, nails about 1-1/2 inches apart.

Skin side of the fish toward the board and nails driven into the wood only far enough to hold firmly but so that they may be pulled easily after cooking. Then sprinkle very generously with rock salt. Store where the draining will not damage anything for exactly eleven hours, then rinse the salt off with fresh water.

Now the fish is ready to cook. Build rack and fire pit so that board may be leaned on rack very nearly vertical about 18 inches from the fire. Use wood for fire with no pitch, and no cedar. Keep fire very low so that the juices of the fish are not cooked out. If the juice starts to run down the boards, cut the fire down or move fish away.

Turn boards end for end occasionally. It should take about three hours to cook if it is a large fish or about two hours for smaller size.

- Bill Fast

Clams on the Half Shell

Let butter clams clean themselves in salt water overnight. Cut clams in half, leave in shell and remove the stomachs. Have griddle medium hot. Grease with bacon fat. Sprinkle clams with crushed cracker crumbs. Season with garlic salt and pepper to taste. Turn clams over with the shell on top and fry until meat is brown and crisp. Serve in shell with lemon slices.

- Thelma Benjestorf, South Beach

School Bus Driver on Guemes

Red Cabbage

1 head red cabbage

2 tablespoon sugar

2 tablespoon bacon fat

Salt and pepper to taste

1 medium onion, minced

Pinch of cloves

2 tablespoon vinegar,

Slice cabbage, put in pot with fat, onion and other ingredients. Cook about 45 minutes to 1 hour.

- Sigrid Trautman, South Beach

Quilter

Green Tomato Mincemeat

1 quart apples, chopped

2 teaspoons cinnamon

1 pint green tomatoes, chopped

1 teaspoon allspice

3 cups sugar

1 teaspoon cloves

1 pound raisins

1/4 cup vinegar

1 teaspoon salt

1. Mix and simmer till thick, then bring to boil and seal.

- Louise Pinneo

Quilter

Eggs A La Maxine

4 to 6 eggs

1/2 cup cream

5-6 green onion, including tops, finely chopped

2 tablespoon butter

1 4-ounce can mushrooms, stems and pieces

Sauté onions and mushrooms in butter until golden. Pour the cream over them until it covers the bottom of the pan to about 1/2 inch. Drop eggs in cream and simmer, covered, until done. Season with salt and pepper and Lawry's seasoning salt.

- Isabelle Griggs

Serves 4

Italiana Meatballs

Chop 3 onions and saute in 1/4 pound salt pork or bacon until clear. Roll 2 pounds ground round steak in balls and brown. Boil and drain 1 large package wide noodles. Combine all and mix with:

2 cans cream corn

1 can solid pack tomatoes

2 cans tomato soup

1/2 pint pitted ripe olives

6 small cans tomato sauce

Add salt, pepper and a dash of chili powder. Bake 1 hour at 350 degrees. Preferably bake the day before and reheat.

- Ruth Tuttle

Serves 20

Green Bean Casserole

1 quart fresh green beans

2/3 cup chopped celery

4 slices bacon, cooked

1 15-ounce can mushroom soup

1 small onion, chopped

Salt and pepper, to taste

Place vegetables in layers. (Note: May be processed for canning this way.) Pour over one can of mushroom soup. Bake at 350 degrees for 1 hour.

- Rosemary Hammill

Horse Ranch

Spinach in Sour Cream Sauce

3 packages spinach, defrosted

1/2 teaspoon salt

1 package onion soup mix

1 1/2 pint sour cream, more as desired

Blend all until smooth, bake in greased casserole at 325 degrees for 20 minutes or until hot throughout.

- Helen Vonnegut

Serves 6-8

Raisin Bread

1 package raisins

2 packages granular yeast

1 1/2 cups milk

1/2 cup warm water

1/2 cup sugar

6 cups flour

1/2 cup shortening

2 teaspoon salt

1 egg

1 teaspoon sugar

1/2 cinnamon

Scald milk. Pour into large bowl. Add sugar, salt and shortening until shortening is melted. Cool to lukewarm and add beaten egg. Crumble yeast into the warm water, stir until dissolved and add to bowl. Add raisins which have been plumped in hot water and drained. Add flour, one cup at a time. Turn out on floured board to knead. Let rise in a warm place about 1 1/2 hours. Divide in 3 and roll out each about the size of pie. Sprinkle with sugar and cinnamon. Roll up like a jelly roll and put in bread pans. Bake at 350 about 45 minutes. Makes 3 loaves.

When cool, can ice with confectioner sugar icing.

- Mrs. Alice Veal

Famous bread maker

Kraut Stuffed Pork Chops

Chop 1 medium onion. Grate 1 large apple and 1 large potato. Mix together with 1 11-ounce can sauerkraut and 2 tablespoons brown sugar.

Salt and pepper 8 chops. Stack chops with dressing between. Skewer or tie together as a roast. Bake in a 350 degree oven for 1 1/2 to 2 hours.

- Gertie and Robert Howard

Guemes Fire Department is named for Robert

Dream Bars

1/2 cup butter

1 cup flour

1/2 cup brown sugar

Mix together to a crumbly mass like piecrust. Pat into a buttered 9x9 pan. Bake at 350 degrees until slightly browned, about 20 minutes.

Mix together:

1 cup brown sugar

1/2 teaspoon baking powder

2 eggs

1/4 teaspoon salt

2 tablespoons flour

1 to 1/2 cup coconut

1 teaspoon vanilla

1/2 to 1 cup chopped walnuts

Pour this over baked mixture. Bake again at 350 degrees until browned 20 to 25 minutes. When cool, cut in bars.

- Virginia Humble

Pineapple Oatmeal Cookies

3/4 cup soft shortening

1 1/2 cups flour, sifted

1 cup brown sugar

1 teaspoon salt

1/2 cup sugar

1 teaspoon baking soda

1 egg

3 cups quick cooking oatmeal

1 teaspoon vanilla

1 cup raisins

1/2 teaspoon cinnamon

1/2 cup chopped walnuts

1/2 teaspoon nutmeg

1 medium can crushed pineapple, drained

Place shortening, sugars, egg and vanilla in mixing bowl and beat thoroughly. Stir in pineapple. Add flour, cinnamon, cloves, nutmeg, soda and salt, mix well. Drop by teaspoonfuls on well greased cookie sheet. Bake in 375 degrees for 15 to 20 minutes.

- Sarah Kingston, family long time residents

Matthews family

Pineapple Fluff

Heat a pound of fresh marshmallows in top of double boiler until melted. Mix with 1 1/2 cups crushed pineapple. Chill in dessert glasses and top with coconut. A light dessert to follow a heavy dinner.

- Mabel Fengler

Makes 6 servings

Rhubarb Conserve

4 cups chopped rhubarb

4 cups sugar

1 cup diced, canned pineapple

Juice of 1/2 lemon

Pulp and grated rind of 1 orange

Cut rhubarb into 1-inch pieces. In a pan, over low heat, slowly cook all ingredients together. Stir frequently to avoid burning. When clear it is done, pour into hot sterile jars and seal.

- Agnes Orsini

Long time North Beach resident

Five-Fruit Marmalade

5 peaches, peeled

1 lemon

5 pears, peeled

1 package pectin

5 apples

Sugar, as needed

1 large orange

Grind all fruit, use 1 cup of sugar for each cup of fruit. Place all in a kettle with pectin and boil until clear and thick. Wonderful on toast.

- Maude Wooten

Matthews family

Never Fail Taffy

2 cups sugar

2/3 cup hot water

1/4 teaspoon cream of tartar

1 tablespoon butter

1 tablespoon vinegar

In a large pan, over low heat, combine all ingredients and stir until sugar dissolves. Then increase heat, cover and boil. Test by putting a little in cold water and it becomes brittle. It is done. Pour in a well buttered pan, let stand until cool enough to pull. Butter hands before starting to pull.

- Hattie Kager

Lee's Devil of a Crab Dip

1 8-ounce package cream cheese

1 tablespoon mayonnaise

2 tablespoons chopped red onion

1/2 teaspoon dry mustard

2 tablespoons chili sauce

3 drops Tabasco hot sauce

1/2 pound Dungeness crab

3 tablespoons chopped green olives

Mix all together in a 8-inch square baking dish. Bake at 375 degrees for 15 minutes. Serve hot, with corn chips.

- Claudia Ashbach

Pickled Herring

6 herring, in brine

Sliced lemon

Onion slices

1 cup white wine vinegar

Bay leaves

1/2 cup white wine

Cayenne

2 tablespoon prepared mustard

1 teaspoon sugar

Prepare herring as above. Place a layer of fish in large dish, add layer of onion, bay leaves, dash of cayennes and layer of lemon slices. Repeat. Mix vinegar, wine, mustard and sugar; pour over fish. Cover and chill for several days.

- Rita Dewar

Treasured Island Recipes Women's Fellowship of Guemes Island Community Church

Compiled by the Women's Fellowship, 1972.

The Quilters

It is to these dedicated and devoted women, it is to them with thankfulness and affection, that we, the Women's Fellowship of the Guemes Island Community Church, dedicate this book.

Within the walls of our little brown church on Guemes Island, the art of quilting has been a firm foundation. For many a year, willing hands, guiding their stitches, have made a thing of beauty. The stitches are made of thread, for the world to see and enjoy. But there is more. For with each movement of the needle, into each linking of the thread, have gone utmost thought of the quilter—the heartbeat, the quiet revelation of a soul, the woven but forever unspoken and unwritten and chapter of a life.

We think of it as "The Little Brown Church on the Island". And so it is. It stands sheltered beneath a forest, ever green. Laurel, Oregon Grape and Rhododendron cluster against its sides. Cattle graze peacefully in an adjacent meadow. It is a small church.

First there was a chapel with a spare kitchen area which, later, was enlarged and equipped with all necessary facilities. After a time a Fellowship room was added and, recently, its size has been doubled.

Each Sunday morning there are few empty seats in the chapel. Members, associates and friends have come to hear the minister and sometimes special music.

Once a month the congregation attends a coffee hour after the service. This social assembly is held in the Fellowship room. In that room, each week, women of the church gather to quilt and to carry on business necessarily helpful to the church. Bible talks are given within the Fellowship and speakers from away frequently come to tell of their work in particular religious and humanitarian fields. From time to time various social events of the church are enjoyed in the Fellowship room.

There have been difficult days too for the church since it was organized sixty-six years ago. Among the early members there was little money and the minister was frequently paid with produce or with quilts made by a group of women known as "The Ladies' Aid".

But through it all there was then--and are now--willing hands and hearts. And there was--and still is--faith.

Today, the little brown church on the island of Guemes stands secure beneath the branches of the ever green forest, a cherished haven, a revered abode.

- Helen Elmore

Caesar Salad

2 slices bread, cubed

1 large head Romaine lettuce, torn

Freshly ground pepper and salt

1 large garlic clove, mashed

3 anchovies, mashed

Dash Worchestershire sauce

1/4 cup red wine vinegar

1 egg yolk, beaten

1/4 cup olive oil

Freshly grated Parmesan cheese

Make garlic croutons by cooking toasted bread cubes in garlic butter. Cool.

In a large salad bowl, mash together pepper, salt, garlic and anchovies. Add Worcestershire sauce and mix well. Mix in wine vinegar, add raw egg yolk and mix well. Add oil and beat with a fork. Toss in the entire romaine and coat leaves well. Grate Parmesan on top and add croutons.

- Anne McCracken

4-6 servings

Sweet and Sour Cabbage Salad

4 cups shredded cabbage

2/3 cup vegetable oil

1 large sweet onion, sliced thin

1 cup vinegar

2 teaspoons sugar

1 teaspoon celery seed

Scant 7/8 cup sugar

Salt, to taste

In a large bowl alternate cabbage and onion. Bring to a boil: vinegar, salt, oil and 2 teaspoons sugar; pour over cabbage and onion. Sprinkle on the 7/8 cup sugar and celery seed. Don't stir. Cover and cool 24 hour in refrigerator. Toss before serving. Drain some of the juice.

- Agnes Ashbach

Serves 6-8

Pesto Genevese

1 cup fresh basil (not dried)

1 tablespoon butter

2 cloves garlic, crushed

1 teaspoon fresh lemon juice

4 tablespoons olive oil

1 tablespoon water

2 tablespoons pinenuts

4 tablespoons grated cheese (half Romano and half Parmesan

Put basil, garlic, 2 tablespoons of oil, pine nuts and water in blender. Blend on low for 1 minute. Add remaining ingredients; blend on low for 30 seconds and then high for 30 seconds. Making into a smooth, thick paste.

Serve on spaghetti, fettucine, or drop a spoonful in a soup or salad dressing.

- Laura Burton

3/4 cup

Roquefort Cheese Dressing

1 cup Best Foods mayonnaise

1/4 pound Roquefort cheese

1/2 cup buttermilk

1 tablespoon Worcestershire sauce

Lemon juice, garlic or onion powder, to taste

Blend all ingredients and chill.

- Meta Whicker

2 cups

Country Fried Rabbit

2-3 pounds tender young rabbit

1 1/2 teaspoons salt

1/2 cup flour

1/4 teaspoon pepper

Butter or shortening

Shake moist pieces of rabbit in a paper bag in mixture of flour, salt and pepper. Place rabbit in 1/4 inch hot butter or shortening (part bacon drippings is good) in heavy skillet, turning to brown evenly on all sides. Remove excess fat from skillet; cover with boiling water. Cover and simmer 1 hour or until tender, turning the rabbit once.

- Vivian Bush

3-6 servings

Charlie Townsend's Favorite Corn Bread

1/2 cup margarine

1/2 teaspoon soda

2/3 cup sugar

1 cup yellow corn meal

2 eggs

1 cup unsifted flour

1 cup buttermilk

1/2 teaspoon salt

Melt margarine in large pan: remove pan from heat and stir in sugar. Add eggs and beat until well blended. Combine buttermilk and soda; stir into mixture. Add corn meal, flour and salt; stir until just blended. Pour into buttered 8-inch square baking pan. Bake at 375 degrees for 30 minutes or until it begins to pull away from sides of the pan.

- Alice Shoultz

1 loaf

Beer Bread

3 1/4 cusp self-rising flour

1/3 cup sugar

1 12-ounce can beer, room temperature

1/2 to 3/4 cup of 'whatever': nuts, raisins, dill weed, wheat germ, etc.

Mix flour and sugar, add beer and stir vigorously. Add 'whatever' and pour into a well-buttered loaf pan. Bake in preheated 375 degree oven 45 to 50 minute. When brown, remove to cooling rack and butter the crust.

- Betty Crookes

1 loaf

Caramel Corn

1 cup brown sugar

1 cube margarine (8 tablespoons)

1/4 cup Karo syrup

3 quarts popped corn

Boil sugar, syrup and margarine to hard-ball stage. Pour over popped corn and stir. Pour onto a buttered jelly roll pan and bake at 250 degrees for 1 hour. Break up immediately; store in plastic bag.

- Jane Veal Read

3 quarts

Refrigerator Bran Muffins

1 1/2 cups sugar

2 1/2 teaspoons soda

1/2 cup vegetable oil

1 cup boiling water

2 eggs

2 cups Kellogg's All-Bran cereal

2 cups buttermilk

1 cup Nabisco All-Bran cereal

2 1/3 cups flour

1 cup raisins

1/2 teaspoon salt

Chopped nuts, optional

Blend together sugar, oil, eggs and buttermilk. Sift together: flour, salt and soda, and stir into egg mixture. In a separate bowl, pour boiling water over the All-Bran cereals, stir and add to mixture. Fold in raisins and nuts. Bake in greased muffin tins 15 to 20 minutes at 400 degrees. Mixture may be kept for several week in the refrigerator, ready to bake.

- Gerry Dutton

About 30 muffins

Peanut Butter Frosting

1/2 cube butter or margarine

1/2-3/4 powdered sugar

4 tablespoons natural peanut butter

Put all ingredients in a mixing bowl; blend by stirring in hot water slowly until it forms a spreadable frosting. If too thin, add more powdered sugar.

Delicious on chocolate cake.

- Helen Trefethen

1 1/2 cups

Sunshine Mashed Potatoes

5 medium peeled potatoes

1 large carrot, scrubbed

3 tablespoons butter

1/4 teaspoon garlic powder

1 teaspoon seasoned salt

1/2 teaspoon onion powder

Milk

Salt and pepper, to taste

Boil carrot and potatoes until just tender; mash and add butter and seasonings. Add milk, as needed, and whip. Garnish with parsley.

- Dessie Weigel

Serves 6

Broccoli Bacon Quiche

2 baked pie shells

2 stalks broccoli, cooked and chopped

1 chopped onion, sautéd

1 cup cooked bacon, crumbled

3 eggs

1/2 teaspoon salt

1 1/2 cup heavy cream

Pinch nutmeg

1/4 teaspoon pepper

1 1/2 cup grated Swiss cheese topping

To make Custard

In a medium bowl, beat eggs and cream. Stir in remaining ingredients.

Sauté broccoli and onion, stir in bacon. Divide between the 2 pie crusts. Pour custard mixture on top and cover with cheese. Bake 30 to 35 minutes at 375 degrees until golden and fluffy.

- Linda Porter

2 pies

Split Second Cookies

"I attest to this recipe, a favorite cookie to make for my family." -Dawn Ashbach

2 cups sifted flour

2/3 cup sugar

1/2 teaspon baking powder

3/4 cup soft butter

1 egg, beaten

2 teaspoons vanilla

Jam or jelly of your choice

Sift together flour, sugar and baking powder. With fingers or forks, blend in butter, egg and vanilla to make a smooth dough. Divide dough into 4 parts, shape each into a roll 13 inches long and 3/4 inch thick. Place on ungreased baking sheet, 4 inches apart and 2 inches from the edges of the sheet. Make a depression, 1/4 to 1/3 inch deep down the center of each roll with a knife handle. Fill the depressions with jam or jelly. Bake at 350 degrees for 15 to 20 minutes. Cut on the diagonal while still warm. Vary the kinds if jam or jelly in each roll for a decorative cookie plate.

- Olive MacFetridge

2 dozen

Lemon Cream Pie

4 egg yolks, beaten

1 cup sugar

4 egg whites

1 baked 9" pie shell

2 tablespoons water

1 teaspoon flour

Zest and juice of 1 large lemon

Cook egg yolks, sugar, lemon zest and juice, water and flour. Cool. Whip 2 egg whites until stiff and fold into cooled egg yolk mixture and pour into pie shell. Make meringue with 2 egg whites. Bake until light brown at 325 degrees.

- Dot Graham

Serves 8

Sugar Cookies

1 cup butter

1 teaspoon vanilla

1 cup shortening

4 1/2 cup flour

1 cup sugar

2 teaspoon cream of tartar

1 cup powdered sugar

2 teaspoons baking soda

3 eggs

1 1/2 teaspoon salt

Cream butter, shortening and the two sugars together. Add eggs and vanilla; beat well. Sift together four, cream of tartar, soda and salt. Blend into the creamed mixture.

Drop by teaspoonful into a bowl with granulated sugar. Then place on a greased cookie sheet, sugared side up. Bake at 350 degrees for 15 minutes.

- Agnes Ashbach

6 dozen

Blueberry Supreme

1 cup powdered sugar

6-ounces blackberry pie filling

1/2 cup butter

1/2 pint whipping cream

2 eggs

1/4 cup pecans

Vanilla wafer crust

Whipped cream

Cream butter and powdered sugar; add eggs one at a time, blending well. Spread mixture over crust and chill. Next, spread blueberry pie filling over chilled mixture and cover with whipped cream. Garnish with chopped pecans and some remaining crumbs.

- Mary M. Stapp

Serves 8

Cooking (giant) crab.

A

F

G

H

Index   217

P

Q

R

S

Index

T

V

W

Y

Z

Contributors

Pat Adams

MJ Andrak

Dawn Ashbach

Dorothy Bird

Bea Cashetta

Yossarian Day

Tara Dowd

Joyce Fleming

Lorraine Francis

Donel Griggs

Mike Hardy

Barbara Hoenselaar

Jan Iversen

Kellie Kalvig

Nancy Lazara

Blake Marckino

Carolyn McCulloch

Joseph Miller

Karon Monahan

Dianne Neilson

Sue Stapp O'Donnell

Julie Pingree

Judy Rainwater

Sue Roberts

Travis Rosenthal

Toni Schmokel

The Seifrieds

Mark Siks

Sally Stapp

Mimi Townsend

Eric Veal

Diane Wallace

Jackie Wittman

Win Anderson

Bud Ashbach

Matt Ashbach

Patricia Bradley

Anne Casperson

Carol Deach

Karen Everett

Deb Flory

Terri Gaffney

Vicki & Chuck Hallingstad

Marietta Harrigan

Mary Holmes

Justin James

Lisa Kennan-Meyer

Diana Lind

Nik Mardesich

David McKibben

Mark and Vicki Mitchell

Miriam Morrison

J. Forrest Nelson

Dawn Orney

Kay Marie Pope

Terri Ramsay Reed

Dave Rockwood

Deanne Savage

Cathy Schoenberg

Gayle and Eddie Selyem

Bonita Smith

Angela Starston

Melita Townsend

Janice Veal

Patsi Waller

Tim Wittman

Elaine Anderson

Lindsay Ashbach

Claudia Ashbach

Nancy Bush

Tyler Clausen

Janice Defosse

Sue Everett

Susie Fox

Ina Garten

Mo Halpin

Dyvon Havens

Sharon Hughlitt

Beverly James

Marge Kilbreath

The Linnemans

Sutheera Marshall

Joan Miller

Allen Moe

Mike Murphy

Renee Norrie

Leo E. Osborne

Lynn Prewit

Pat Richley-Erikson

Bruce Rooney

Wendy Savers

Laurie Scott

Meghan Sheridan

Syd Stapleton

Carol Steffy

Bill Van Vlack

Edith Walden

Kathy Whitman

Yadira Young

Made in the USA
Middletown, DE
22 August 2024

59040503R00126